LEADING LIKE A WOMAN

FUNDI NZIMANDE

ISBN: 9798593440013

Acknowledgements

I would not have had the know-how to write this book without my great grandmothers, Gertrude MaNgobese Guma and Margaret MaHlongwa Magubane as well as my grandmother Busisiwe KaMagubane Guma and my aunt Phiwase MaGuma Dlamini who was the first to employ me as a development consultant. I would not have had the language without Phakamile Guma, my mother, who was my first dedicated English teacher and my father Mandla "Khalulu" Nzimande who paid the Varsity fees even when it really hurt!

I would not have completed its writing without my cheerleaders: my cousins Musa and Thandeka Dlamini, my aunt Phumelele Msweli, my friend Jabu Mbatha and my mentor Debby Edelstein.

I acknowledge the spiritual guidance and strengthening from my church, the Ministry of Christ Embassy and all in my spiritual family.

I acknowledge all those individuals and institutions who gave me space to learn about leadership in the NGO, Women's, Trade Union Movements.

I acknowledge all the writers who have written before me and all my dedicated teachers and lecturers from Primary School to University.

I thank you all from the bottom of my heart!

Preface

Leadership is one of the most important pursuits of our lifetimes. It is a pursuit that needs to be undertaken consciously, cautiously and with great care as it affects people's lives, interests, expectations and benefits. It is an activity that requires intellect, vision, insight, intuition, self-awareness, awareness of the environment and group dynamics, a great deal of love and patience for people and emotional intelligence.

In many societies leadership has been, for centuries, the preserve of men. What we have been led to understand today is that the different stages of human development have been characterized by communalism in the early stages. In that stage, all individuals worked as a collective to ensure the survival of the collective. The communal stage was also characterized by the same standard of living for the entire communal village. There were no rich or poor women (men). Food and other necessities for survival were shared equally. Groups of women worked together as gatherers and nurturers whilst groups of men worked together as hunters. This data has been gathered by anthropologists and interpreted by historians and political scientists.

With the development of human society, distinctions between the haves and have-nots emerged because of traditions that developed out of ownership and "mine" (often referred to as monopolization of public goods) which set those who own apart from those who do not own. Because of this development, distinctions emerged between the rich and the poor and they also began to set apart the men from the women and this calcified in the feudal age where women became completely disempowered as they were now fully the property of men with no voice at all. In Africa this was different because in the stage at which Africans intersect with other continents, women still had relative importance as the providers of food and healing who worked the land without impediments. In some of these African societies, women could lead (as queens and regents) and could also go to war as soldiers. They could also participate in the communal meetings.

Most of the voicelessness that still plagues African women in the twenty-first century is mostly resulting from Africa's interactions with other cultures of the East as well as the North who had (through their social, political and economic systems) taken away woman's agency with only a few notable exceptions in history.

The leadership activity has thus been male-dominated in many societies and in all continents, except for a few cultures that did not interact with Europe or Asia at specific points in history. The challenges of intransigent and endemic inequality have led women to organize themselves to challenge these injustices. These organizations and women have been informed by a range of approaches that have been individualistic (liberal) to others that have been more collective and systemic (radical and socialist).

In some cases, these feminists have been able to get the support of men and to place their agenda in the multilateral institutions to a point where we speak of gender equality and gender mainstreaming for a more just and fairer world. In these discussions, it has become clear that women's agency, voice and leadership should be encouraged so that women can be part of the solutions to the problems that affect them, their communities and the world at large.

The systems namely: social, political and economic that have been developed over time have been extremely violent to women. They allowed for the super-exploitation of women, the abuse of women, the dispossession and impoverishment of women as well as the negation of women. At the same time, these systems have not allowed recourse to women in the justice systems of the world. This has been starker in the developing world whilst in the developed world justice has been too expensive for women to seek and get recourse. The NGOs that have emerged to support justice for women have not been enough to stem the flood of injustices experienced by women in the home, the community and the economy.

The experience of this author has confirmed with only one variation out of fifteen women leaders experienced, that women leaders are confident and clear about the direction that they want to take in leadership. They have **not** used lies and manipulation to get things done. They have been vulnerable and transparent. They have been consultative. They have not been afraid to receive feedback, proposals and suggestions. I have also witnessed that women support other women leaders in only three cases out of those fifteen cases. It occurred to me that perhaps a contribution to the topic of leader- ship and gender could contribute in advancing the discussion and the practice in leadership and around leadership.

This book has also been inspired by the disregard, neglect, underdevelopment and discouragement of woman leadership in all spheres of life. This has been coupled with lack of support of woman leaders by other women (more on this in the first chapter), and a more visceral and violent silencing or management of emerging women's voices that sought to raise the injustices meted out to women and other groups of people such as youth, the disabled, non-white, indigenous and gender non-conforming people. This silencing has come from varied combinations of patriarchy, capitalism and racism.

The book has noted and been driven by the research findings that show that, whilst women's numbers are slowly increasing in the leadership and management of institutions, their influence cannot be said to be increasing commensurately (Please see chapter dealing with the Non-Profit sec- tor to get an indication of what is meant by this paradoxical situation). These points to a need for consciously increasing women's numbers as well as in- creasing women's influence and impact (transformation) in different institutions.

This author believes strongly that the difference of gender dynamics between men and women, which comes about mostly because of gendered identity that develops from the mode of socialization, is what gives women the edge in successful leadership. The fact that women, especially in the developing world, are raised to be all-rounded human beings who can be nannies, care- givers, educators, comforters, nurses/ healers, religious leaders, cooks, housekeepers, finance managers, disciplinarians, mentors etc in the home is the very reason that makes them so suitable for a wide range of social roles and make such a great impact in leadership, when they finally ascend to it.

The only downside to this preparation is that it is coupled with malevolent undermining and attacking of any contribution of women, inter alia, in the home, the workplace, the community, and political spaces. Men, be- cause of the lofty roles that society imagines for them, do not get a chance to develop their humane sides properly and often, are thrust into leadership before they mature. Admittedly, this is a generalization; because there are clear indications of exceptions to the gender differences between men and women, not least gender non-conforming individuals.

Women who participated in the Women Matter Africa study by McKinsey & Company of August 2016 also indicated that the following factors accounted for their success:

Robust work ethic: Go above and beyond what is expected. Many developed this work ethic in response to gender bias, that is, they felt they had to work twice as hard as their male peers from early in their careers.

Persistence in achieving goals and willingness to take risks: Set specific goals, work toward them, and set new ones as soon as they are achieved. For some, the willingness to take risks (a quality they saw as uncommon among female peers) – by entering male-dominated industries or environments, applying for jobs above the current level, and changing jobs in pursuit of growth opportunities was essential to achieving their leadership goals.

Resilience in the face of adversity: Cultivate a veneer of toughness, refuse to take setbacks personally, have the courage to dissent.

Commitment to professional development: Proactively seek career opportunities and ways to improve as a professional.

Mentors, sponsors and peer networks: Build a group of male and female mentors and sponsors inside and outside the organization as a forum for honesty, feedback, and self-reflection; actively mentor juniors and encourage other senior women to do the same.”

These factors make the argument for woman leadership and this book more compelling. At the same time, they make the argument for encouraging more women to take up leadership necessary because this shows that not every woman is prepared to take risks and persist in a male-dominated field such as leadership. It also makes a powerful argument for transforming organizations and institutions to become inclusive places and friendly places for women (and any other marginalized group).

This book seeks to add to the discussion, thinking and further conceptualization about the kind of leadership we need for a much fairer and just world considering the length of time, the centuries that women and other discriminated groups have been subjugated in a patriarchal, male-dominated world. The practice of "leading like a woman" can be adopted by anyone, male, female or other. It begins to challenge the patriarchal style of leadership and to suggest a suite of leadership styles for leadership towards a more just and fairer world. This book also attempts to consciously write from a female-centered perspective to challenge androcentrism in our literature.

The people who will benefit from this book are leaders, decision-makers, activists, influencers and women from all walks of life.

Chapter 1: Leadership and Gender

The system of male domination (patriarchy) that has developed over thousands of years is still very endemic in our societies including the most advanced of human societies where a backlash is always experienced with conservative elements seeking to haul back the gains made by women and other dominated groups in those societies. The character of patriarchy has fostered interesting gender relations between men and women where authority and power has been and/or is reserved for men, where there is inequality between men and women that favors men. It has elicited a division of labor between men and women where women play a bigger (if not a sole) role in domestic (reproductive) work and where men play a bigger role (if not a sole role) in the public sphere including the role of leadership. The issue of men and women's role in reproductive work varies in different societies be- cause of the struggle for women's liberation/ emancipation. In some societies more and more men take responsibility for reproductive work to a point where some men have chosen to be house husbands or "home executives". The traditional role of men as those who play a public role is often characterized by a higher appointment or election rate of men over women for positions of management and leadership.

The system of male domination in leadership has been hetero-normative and visible with most companies, political parties, trade unions, religious institutions, education institutions, judicial institutions and so on dominated by men in leadership. This has meant that women's concerns have not been understood and have sometimes been trivialized by people who have no idea how it feels to be rendered a non-factor in decision-making and an over- whelmed bearer of all of society's ills.

Male-domination in these institutions is often exacerbated by other factors such as race where people who are not white have been subjected to the worst forms of patriarchy in both private and public spaces reducing constitutional promises of most countries to a lie. It has also been exacerbated by the age factor where young women and girl-children have been subjected to horrific expressions of patriarchy because of their sex and/or age. It has al- so been worsened by the disability factor where disabled women have been either neglected, forgotten and subjected to the worst forms of human abuse because of their disability and sex.

It has also been exacerbated by economic factors where poor women have been treated as things and tools by systems and men because of their economic position and sex. Geography and history have also come in to play their role here. If one is a woman in any of the developing countries, chances are public services are hard to access. If one is living in a previously colonized society, chances are, if you are a woman your struggle for equality is more difficult than the struggle for equality of a European woman; but even when you migrate to the Northern countries you take that position and condition with you. Where one is a young, poor, disabled, black African woman the reports of abuse and exploitation make any sane and compassionate human being shudder.

Weaving through all this is the very common collusion between the authorities in the economy, politics and judiciary; making it nigh impossible for ordinary (read poor and middle class) women to access the justice that is due to them, in the home, from the state and from the economy.

The issue of women's leadership is important, but not only by itself. The systems also need to change, to be forced to accommodate all and be inclusive. The leaders who are women, men and other all need to be conscientised about issues of gender dynamics and the inequality of power and authority between men, women and other. Because patriarchy is so endemic many, many women are themselves the gatekeepers for patriarchy, are patriarchal and unconsciously so.

No woman sets out to be patriarchal, but many factors collude to make women very patriarchal. One of these factors is how we interpret or under- stand religious text. It is this author's belief that it is men who infuse gender inequality and a non-spiritual element into the religious texts. Another factor that makes women patriarchal is the understanding of culture. Culture is created and sustained by human beings, which means that we should be able to change any culture that does not serve us. Culture is said to be dynamic, that it changes over time. Another factor that makes women patriarchal is fear. Women have many reasons to be fearful such as Gender Based Violence in the home, the community, the education system, the economy etc.

Another reason for women to be fearful is lack of economic security. Whatever the cause of the fear, it can make women very patriarchal in relation to their sons' wives, other women leaders, women colleagues and fellows in religious institutions, women fellows in the education institutions, women fellows in the community, women fellows in their relationship with one man and so on and so on. Job-insecurity can make women patriarchal as, often; men are in charge in the workplace. Insecurity in the union because, often; men are in charge in the union. Insecurity in the political party because, often; men are in charge in the political party. Basically, wherever women go they are outnumbered and outweighed in the authority stakes which causes them to be inadvertently patriarchal. It is this fear and negotiating patriarchy and misogyny that make women unable or unwilling to form or join women-founded political parties even when the evidence for doing so could be compelling.

The factors that contribute to patriarchy are societal. As societies have developed historically, male-domination has become entrenched and calcified. Patriarchy has become endemic and all-pervasive to the extent that men and women have patriarchal traits to varying degrees. The exercise of seeking justice for those who are oppressed by patriarchy challenges even the victims of patriarchy themselves, because patriarchy dominates ways of seeing, ways of thinking and ways of doing. Even feminists and gender activists are susceptible to patriarchal traits and must constantly apply introspection as they continue with transformative interventions.

That means that part of the time men themselves are not consciously being patriarchal. It is just what they have learnt and internalized during socialization and this can be referred to as, "second nature". Part of the time men are consciously patriarchal. In those times, they are doing everything they can to plot against the idea of woman leadership and the emerging reality of woman leadership. They hold secret meetings and caucuses to impede the advancement towards gender balance in leadership and the work of women leaders.

They take the decision-making away from the Boardroom or formal meeting to male spaces such as male bathrooms, male clubs in those societies that still have these and into the golf courses where very serious decisions that affect hundreds, thousands, millions and billions of people locally and worldwide are taken. These ways of doing leadership are distinctively male and exclusionary and perpetuate inequalities within and outside the Boardroom. In environments that are dominated by women, male and patriarchal leaders use personal attacks and humiliation to deal with individuals and this works very well to silence people, as no-one wants to be in the spot- light and risk public humiliation. They also use divide and rule where they promote certain groups of women who will stand in opposition to other women who are demanding equality and fairer conditions. These challenges can and have been overcome in some environments and activists must be encouraged to keep chipping away at gender discrimination, gender inequality and patriarchy.

Patriarchal styles of leadership have a particularly vicious way of dealing with being challenged. Most of the time the justification for a chosen course of action for a patriarchal leader comes from a fearful place and when it is challenged, the fear of exposure compounds its fearful origins.

Chapter 2: Leading like a woman can incorporate "Ubuntu"

1. Introduction

Leading like a woman can integrate cultural awareness. Many cultures in the developing world have had some form of communalism and collective approaches and pro-people values and as such the best aspects of these cultures that resonate with a human rights-based legal framework can be integrated. In this chapter "Ubuntu" is mentioned to illustrate the point.

2. What is "Ubuntu"?

"Ubuntu" in a simple way is humaneness or the ability to be humane. This has been a way of life for Southern Africans since pre-colonial times. "Ubuntu" means that a person cares for all people in their community. It is about warmth towards each other. It is about checking on your neighbors often. It is about sharing what we have with one another. In an "Ubuntu" framework you cannot eat when your neighbor does not have. In fact, you will not eat if a person in your space is not eating. When you are hungry, you will eat your food only by sharing it. "Ubuntu" allows for you to give and for your neighbor to be able to come and ask for something. In this frame the things we ask for are for survival. When your neighbor is ill, and you have a phone, you can call the ambulance. Sometimes you just take care of her until she is well, as the situation requires. In the Nguni culture there is a saying, "umuntu ngumuntu ngabantu" which means "a person is a person because of others" meaning you will not bear your burdens alone, others will always be there to carry them with you. It means my humanity is reflected in your humanity and vice versa. It means that if you are undergoing difficulty, I am also undergoing difficulty and vice versa.

This belief system of "Ubuntu" weaved through everything such as:

- When your family is small, the village pitches in to help you work your fields or when you are new to our settlement, the village pitches in to help you build your homestead.

- There is very little individualism, me, myself and I in "Ubuntu.

- When you refresh your grass roof, we pitch in to help. When you are building an additional room, we pitch in to help.

- When you have travelled from a faraway place, we give you food and a place to sleep. We do not need to know who you are before we can help you.

- When you are coming to settle with your small family, you are taken to the king and the king will give you some start-up cattle and chickens, male and female and some land on which to settle. You are integrated into our community. We do not investigate your motives for moving from your previous location.

- All children are our children which mean anyone can discipline your children. You cannot ignore any "foolishness" that your neighbor's child is doing. You must correct him there and then.

- When the young women go to the river to get water or to get wood from the forest; they go together as a group.

- It also means that we respect and honors each other as creatures of the Creator. This is shown by greeting everyone you meet on the path or in a gathering. A young person defers to an older person who is seen as the bearer of wisdom. It means listening deeply and in a meaningful, interested manner to another person when they speak. It means thinking deeply about your response in a conversation. It means protecting another person's feelings as if they were your own, by affirming them and avoiding exchanges that will embarrass or humiliate them.

- It also means that in relationships between men and women, men honor women as bearers of life and healers. In a marriage there is a saying that, "Umfazi ushelwa zonke izinsuku" which means that you must charm your wife everyday as in those days when you still sought to build a relationship with her. Another saying was, "awukho umuzi owakhiwa ngenduku" meaning "no home can ever be built on domestic violence" letting you know, domestic violence was an issue, per- haps not as widespread nor as horrific, even in pre-colonial times. It also lets you know that everyone would be in your business, including in your inability to relate to women with a soft touch.

- Children and young people do not make noise around elders and groups of children and young people gathered separately from the elders except in the dancing section of any good party or wedding.

- It means keeping your word. This was made easy by the fact that a simple exchange between two people is not rushed. You take time to discuss even the most mundane things, so you won't be trapped into a promise made hastily. In this frame, nothing is ever rushed; decision making is a truly slow and well-considered process.

- It means not seeking recognition and awards, but humbly receiving recognition and awards when they are given. This means that, in the "ubuntu" frame, you cannot promote yourself even when it is evident how great you are. Your promotion and your recognition must come from the world around you.

- In the "ubuntu" frame, you do not stare people in the eye. This is considered very rude. You cast your eye around a person, you incline your head towards a person; but you do not stare them in the eye. (This is so interesting because it has been the source of many-a-contestation between Europeans and Africans because these cultures interpret this practice in diametrically opposed ways).

"Ubuntu" is the opposite of Western traditions of individualism and the utilitarian ways in which people are used and sometimes discarded as it so often happens in mass retrenchments. The Western and capitalist ways have impacted the culture of the African people and distorted many of the traditions that served the African communities at the time into something completely unbearable, especially for women.

It is a real possibility that at the height of the "ubuntu" belief system, most citizens reaped benefits from it. Most of the challenges with the system seem to develop at the point of intersection with Europeans, in Southern Africa. This belief system crumbled under new influences and new material conditions.

3. "Ubuntu", Human Rights and Gender Equality

It goes without saying that we need to stretch the concept of ubuntu where we think it was open to misuse by unethical people in the case of, for example, children. They are expected to defer to elders, not to "talk back" to elders when opinions differ, and women had to learn to "stay in their place" with the transition from communalism to feudalism to industrialized societies. In the frame of "ubuntu", our interconnectedness touches on children, youth, the disabled, LGBTI, women etc. If we recognize our interconnectedness, it means we recognize that our well-being depends on each other's wellbeing. This, then, means that human rights and gender equality can sit comfortably with "ubuntu". This is a highly simplified submission on the topic, but scholars of human rights law can assist in studying this field further.

4. "Ubuntu" and leadership in the current period

A leader who is leading like a woman must be a good listener. She must value the input of her team members. This does not mean that she does not apply her mind to any recommendation; but that she must consider all proposals seriously and be able to take the best proposals. A leader who is leading like a woman must nurture her team. Help the team members to grow into leadership as well. This is done by supporting them where they need support and coaching of team members comes in handy here.

A leader who is leading like a woman reminds the team often about the vision, the mission and the company values which promotes a professional and collegial atmosphere. A leader who is leading like a woman recognizes the humanity of a team member and treats sensitive feedback sessions with confidentiality. She avoids giving negative feedback in the open where anyone can hear and use that confidential information against that team member.

A leader who leads like a woman affirms her team members, even more so, if they lack confidence. This includes a caring manner that the leader uses to engage with her team, considering the individual circumstances of each member.

Chapter 3: Leading like a woman must incorporate transformational leadership

1.0 What is transformational leadership?

In short, transformational leadership is a leadership style that is directed at instituting change in individuals and change in social systems. This style of leadership incorporates a range of actions and interventions to transform followers or members of a led group into leaders. It is also the most suitable style to embrace when one is seeking change in a social system. When transformational leadership is used in its purest form it incorporates mechanisms that build up existing motivation or instills motivation, builds up the morale and performance of the led group members. Transformational leaders connect the inherent capabilities and self of identity of the members to the mission at hand and to the whole collective identity of the organization or institution. It calls on the leaders to be role-models. The leader must challenge the members of the led collective to take greater ownership for their contribution to the mission at hand. Transformational leadership is a demanding activity because it calls on leaders to identify the strengths and weaknesses of the led collective the better to deploy them to tasks that take the mission forward.

The transformational leader works with members of the collective to identify the change that needs to happen. The transformational leader is a revolutionary of sorts as they work with collectives to change those things that need to change for the success of the mission. The vision is created jointly with the team and the leader must continue providing inspiration and consistently work towards the mission together with *committed* members. In this process the leader is working with the committed members and doing troubleshooting (more on this in the Chapter on "Leading like a woman is tough").

"The concept of transformational leadership is based on the leader's personality, traits and ability to make a change through example, articulation of an energizing vision and challenging goals. The extent to which a leader is transformational is measured first, in terms of (her) influence on the followers. These outcomes occur because the transformational leader offers followers something more than just working for self-gain; they provide followers with an inspiring mission and vision and give them an identity. The leader transforms and motivates followers through his or her idealized influence (earlier referred to as charisma), intellectual stimulation and individual consideration. In addition, this leader encourages followers to come up with new and unique ways to challenge the status quo and to alter the environment to support being successful." (http://www.langston.edu/ }

Role modeling

The transformational leader seeks to advance the performance level of her team. When she allocates tasks to her team, she must also perform the task and show how team members can do it and she also encourages team members to be innovative in their execution of the task.

Case Study:

A leader got a position at a Community College. The Community College had an agreement with a University to offer part of its programs. The College was seeking to develop its team to be able to develop learning programs that could be accredited at a Higher Education Level and had to, therefore, start developing learning programs that could be accredited through the University's arrangements so that later, these could be owned by the Community college and accredited by the Higher Education Level. The leader developed material for two of the learning programs using various sources to do so and shared the methodology and the end-product with her team. The result of this exercise was that one of her team members was able to do this.

Later the team leader taught these modules under the auspices of the University and so did the other team member. In the following year two other team members were able to teach some of the programs under the auspices of the University.

In the case study above the team leader was able to identify the strengths of the team and to sense that the team members had the potential to under- take this task, but they were held back by fear. The team member who developed the material and taught under the auspices of the University in the first year was a male. The two team members who taught the second year were female. The team leader worked with the two men to build their confidence levels and they executed the task excellently. The environment of the Community college was very patriarchal and humiliation and subtle threats were used to make the women feel incapable and afraid, but through persistence patriarchy was defeated in that particular instance.

Future vision

Transformational leaders often make use of facilitators and consultants to facilitate the process of reviewing the past, what has worked in the past, what has not worked in the past and to set a new vision or to affirm the existing organizational/ institutional vision. This process needs the participation of all team members. If the team is small, tasks towards setting or affirming the vision may be done individually and collated in a group discussion. If the team is big these tasks can be undertaken in smaller groups and collated in the bigger group. In the process of collation, the group can select the most resonant aspects and draw it into a vision.

This process may be a once-off event or taken in stages. What is critical is that once this vision is set or affirmed, the leader has to refer to it and cement it in the minds of the collective.

The vision is accompanied by a mission statement and a planned programme of implementation that seeks to push the vision forward. The leader draws the team's attention to the vision often and causes members to evaluate themselves and the team in line with the agreed vision, the agreed mission statement and the agreed programme of action.

Individual support

The leader must ensure that all the resources that are required for execution are made available. The leader cannot expect people to offer the best service or the best product if the resources required to produce this product or this service are not available. This is the first step towards supporting one's team members. Financial resources are key in the execution of most missions. It is very discouraging to the team when a transformational leader is seen to be forging ahead with the mission and yet the team members see only failure ahead because they know that there are no financial resources to execute the tasks at hand.

Case Study:

In one organization the leader and the team were working on a huge project. The project would, if successfully implemented, have a huge impact on the sector. The catch was the successful execution of the project would depend on a huge outlay of capital and the budget of the organization did not cover these costs. The leader knocked on several doors and managed to raise even more funds to execute the project with three weeks to spare towards the due date.

In the case study above, we can see that the leader did not inspire the same faith that she had into her team. The team needed to be rallied around the plan for securing the resources for the project.

The transformational leader must have time or a plan for the support of individual members. In high intensity environments, the support for individual members can be facilitated by outside institutions. That calls for financial resources to be available for this type of intervention and this intervention does not take away from the leader to be available for her immediate subordinates to provide individual support to them so that they can execute their tasks. This allows the leader to track their performance and to provide guidance and feedback to her team. Transformational leaders can schedule monthly one-on-one meetings with their immediate subordinates for this support and could have additional one-on-one meetings if so required.

This support helps the leader immensely as she gets to walk in tandem with her immediate team and this helps prepare the team mentally or to adjust mentally for the vision which almost always requires new ways of thinking, new ways of working and a higher output and impact.

Promotion of group goals

a) Participatory Methods

Leaders who want to promote group goals use participatory methods that include everyone. This way when the goals are set, the team gets to own them because they were developed together.

b) Simplify

Simplifying relates to the language the leader uses. The leader must stay away from jargon unless she is prepared to explain the jargon several times as this helps to elevate the team depending on the environment.

Simplifying also relates to the goals. They must be kept simple and yet specific. This may mean you set fewer goals that have maximum impact for the organization or institution. This is critical in institutions that may have re- source constraints.

c) Recognize and celebrate great ideas and performance

In the group/ team meetings invite ideas from the team and incorporate them in the execution of the vision if they are good ideas and remind every- one whose idea that was.

Where team members reach their targets early or particularly well, draw everyone's attention to this and celebrate this with the team.

d) The vision must always be in your sights

The vision can be refreshed or affirmed together. The key is to remind every- one, every chance you get where the team is going, what the vision is. Members must always identify with and take pride in the vision of the organization/institution.

e) **Prioritize together**

Promoting our goals may mean we prioritize certain things and sacrifice certain things. It is always better if we can sacrifice together and the best ex- ample of this is sacrificing time together, not just the team sacrificing, but the leader must sacrifice as well. This is very important as in many businesses and institutional spaces most of the sacrifice is expected from team members except for the team leader.

f) **Coach your immediate team consistently**

The team needs to be coached on an ongoing basis and supported in a similar fashion. This allows the team members to raise challenges that a leader can guide members on towards resolution. It also means that the team leader can share more with team members about the vision and the strategic considerations attached to the vision during the coaching sessions.

g) **Be genuine**

Transformational leadership and promotion of group goals must be a genuine exercise. This means that a transformational leader is not afraid to be vulnerable. This is easy for women and discriminated groups to do. In our socialization process we have taught boys over a very long time that "boys don't cry." The transformation that needs to happen will affect everyone: male, female or other.

h) **Ongoing Inspiration**

The leader must always work on inspiring the team to do better and to do more and achieve greater impact. Teams are inspired by high ideals, a leader who works shoulder to shoulder with them, a leader who provides opportunities for self-development, a leader who says, "thank you" and "that was really great" and a leader who is a role model. Don't ask your team to do something you won't/can't do. This works against the intended outcomes.

Intellectual stimulation

Intellectual stimulation can take several forms. These can include:

- Inviting certain experts to talk to the team

- Allocating (arranging) funding and opportunity for team members to study further

- Hold discussions about topical issues relevant to the team

- Arrange Seminars or send your team to relevant Seminars

High performance expectation

Team members must know that high performance is expected, and team members must be encouraged to reach higher rungs of performance. Team members who exhibit high performance must be celebrated. The key is for the team to improve consistently. Care must be taken that members get the necessary support to avoid burnout under such conditions.

Chapter 4: Leading Like a Woman can be Situational

1. Introduction

Situational leadership is leadership style that adapts to varying situations within the context of leadership. It is a style of leadership that combines different styles of leadership in an organization or institution, usually a work setting. This strategy involves assessing team members in terms of their skills, competencies, levels of confidence and commitment to the organization. It also involves weighing many variables in the workplace and choosing the leadership style that best fits their goals and circumstances at a given time. This leadership style acknowledges that it is best to use it in a work- place.

The bedrock of Situational Leadership is adaptability. Situational leadership is about modifying the style of leadership or management to address the specific requirements of the organization.

There are two models of Situational Leadership, one described by Daniel Goleman

and another by Ken Blanchard and Paul Hersey.

2. Situational Leadership according to Daniel Goleman

Daniel Goleman wrote "Emotional Intelligence." He defines six approaches within situational leadership.

1. **Coaching leaders**- seek to contribute to the personal development of their team members as well as the skills and competencies of team members that are required by their job or employment contract. This style works best with people who are self-aware, are aware of their limitations and are willing to grow.

Case Study:

In a Non-profit workplace, the Executive Manager implemented Coaching to all the Managers of Departments that reported to her. Coaching worked well with two managers who felt that they needed to grow in certain areas and had a higher commitment to the institution. Coaching did not work well with another Manager who felt that he did not need coaching and was in denial about his personal limitations.

In this case study, the Executive Manager did not assess the Manager correctly and thought/assumed that she shared common goals with the Man- ager. This assumption proved problematic as the Manager ultimately had to be assisted with more issues than initially expected and he was still in denial about the need for assistance with developing management skills as well as numerous other personal issues. This example indicates that the assessment of candidates for management and for further coaching needs to be more stringent in all workplaces.

It could help to develop guides about the leadership qualities that are needed and to assess potential leaders based on these in workplace contexts.

2. **Pacesetting leaders**- these leaders set very high expectations for them- selves and their team members. They never ask team members to do anything that they would not do themselves. They lead by example. This style helps to expose leadership quality for high intensity workplaces. It may also lead to burn out, so it must be used with care, if at all. Care here can investigate how time-off and shorter days can be given to workers during those periods in which the organization is not busy.

3. **Democratic leaders**- These leaders give followers a vote in most decisions. It is the best style to use in developing or reviewing the organizational vision, mission and strategic plans. Under optimal conditions, it can build community, collegiality and ownership of decisions within the group. The democratic approach is ideal for certain tasks within the organization; but it is extremely unsuitable during project implementation where deadlines are tight, as it is time-consuming.

Affiliative leaders- these leaders put employees first. This style is only used when morale is very low. The leader uses praise and helpfulness to build up the team's confidence. This style may expose the organization to the risk of poor performance when team building is being implement-ed. This means long hours for Management to close exposure to poor performance.

4. **Authoritative leaders**- these leaders are very confident, they are very good at analyzing problems and identifying challenges. This style is good in an organization that is not meeting its targets, that is underperforming or that is in crisis mode. This leader may or may not allow his or her followers to help figure out how to solve a problem.

5. **Coercive leaders**- these leaders tell their subordinates what to do. They have a very clear vision of the result and how to reach it. This style is good only in times of crisis or if an organization requires a total makeover.

3. Situational Leadership according to Blanchard and Hersey:

Situational leadership according to Blanchard and Hersey must be used for specific types of team members as follows:

Leadership Approach	Type of Team Member
Telling leaders = (specific guidance and close supervision): These leaders make decisions and communicate them to others. They create the roles and objectives and expect others to accept them. Communication is usually one way. This style is most effective in a disaster or when repetitive results are required.	**Level M1:** Followers have low competence and low commitment.
Selling = (explaining and persuading): These leaders may create the roles and objectives for others, but they are also open to suggestions and opinions. They "sell" their ideas to others to gain cooperation.	**Level M2:** Followers have low competence, but high commitment.
Participating = (sharing and facilitating): These leaders leave decisions to their followers. Although they may participate in the decision-making process, the ultimate choice is left to employees.	**Level M3:** Followers have high competence, but low commitment and confidence.
Delegating = (letting others do it): These leaders are responsible for their teams but provide minimum guidance to workers or help to solve problems. They may be asked from time to time to help with decision- making.	**Level M4:** Followers have high competence and high commitment and confidence.

4. Characteristics of Situational Leaders

- **Insight:** This is a very important characteristic of a situational leader. The leader must be able to have accurate insight into the members of her team to use a suitable leadership style.

- **Adaptability:** Situational leaders must be very flexible and adaptable to change leadership styles at a moment's notice to emerge with a suitable leadership style as per situation and/or team member.

- **Trust:** The leader must be trust worthy as far as the team members are concerned.

- **Problem solving:** The situational leader must have well -developed problem-solving skills that utilize a range of leadership styles to get problems solved.

- **Coach:** The coaching characteristic is highly dependent on insight. The situational leader must be able to provide coaching to team members that will enhance their competencies and skills as well as their personal development.

5. Situational Leadership Pros and cons

Pros	Cons
<ul><li>Easy to use and adaptable: When a leader has the right style, he or she knows it</li><li>Simple: All the leader needs to do is evaluate the situation and apply the correct leadership style</li><li>Intuitive appeal: With the right type of leader, this style is comfortable</li><li>Leaders have permission to change management styles as they see fit</li></ul>	<ul><li>This North American style of leader- ship does not take into consideration priorities and communication styles of other cultures</li><li>It ignores the differences between female and male managers (male- centered)</li><li>Situational leaders can divert attention away from long-term strategies and politics</li></ul>

Source: https://courses.lumenlearning.com

5. Benefits of Situational Leadership

The style is highly adaptable. It relies on an accurate assessment of the situation and the team members and adapting the leadership style as suitable. It relies on the situation as opposed to the inherent skills of the leader/ manager as this style is found suitable for workplaces.

Chapter 5: Leading like a woman means you must be attuned to the needs of your people

1. Introduction

Leadership is inherited, bestowed, or taken.

Inherited leadership means one is born into leadership as in a royal house- hold. When leadership is inherited, the person born into leadership may be groomed for leadership and they may learn all the right things about leader- ship and even improve the leadership of a royal family. The opposite canal so be true in that a person born into leadership may not have the capacity to be groomed into leadership as in the case of someone who has little or no emotional intelligence. This may be the case also because they take their position of inherited leadership for granted and may not feel a compunction to perform in the task of leadership, because it has always been in the family and there is an expectation that no matter how poorly one performs the task of leadership, nothing will change; the family's leadership will always be assured.

This is one of the reasons that inherited leadership as the sole type of leadership has collapsed in many parts of the globe. Where inherited leader- ship still exists, it is mostly supplemented with some form of collective/ democratic leadership. How these two types of leadership co-exist in some form of democratic political dispensation, in terms of the depth and genuine nature of democracy varies from nation to nation.

Bestowed leadership means one's leadership is either an appointment or an election. When a leader is appointed, this is usually linked to some form of performance contract that is formalized, although there are still spaces where the performance is not formalized, and the assessment is done informally using broad and often arbitrary standards to measure performance. When a leader is elected, the performance expectation is usually not categorical nor specified. In simple terms, you remain in leadership for as long as you are willing and the people who elected you still like you. Elected leadership may or may not be evaluated in terms of that institution/ organization's resolutions and policies; but outside factors outside the organization can be brought into the evaluation, for example; if the media does not like you, your chances of maintaining your position are slim to none.

Taken leadership means the leadership is an election (preceded by a leadership contest/ election campaign) or that one assumes a leadership role or that it is taken in a coup. An elected person can take leadership if their campaign is run on the issues that matter the most to people (more on this in this chapter). When one assumes a leadership role it usually means that the leadership role is played by an unofficial leader when there is a vacuum or when official leadership is ineffective. In such cases, the leader is recognized by the people in the organization as the real leader of that organization/ institution.

Leadership that is taken in a coup exists, but this brief introduction will not focus on that as it is often very problematic in the con- text of promoting transparency, agreed governance systems, teamwork and collectives in leadership.

2.0 The importance of being attuned

Some of the most successful leaders in history have been so because they led by listening. Listening to the members of your team is one of the most important things you will do as a leader. When a leader listens to the members of the team, this helps to build a meaningful relationship between the leader and her team. Many people in different work (and other relevant) spaces are looking for validation that their contribution is valued and the way in which they get to know that their contribution is valued, is through being listened to, really listened to.

Listening meaningfully and being attuned to your team is not an easy thing to do. It involves self-control. This means the leader listens fully, without interrupting. When the leader is listening fully, she is not listening with one ear and preparing a quick response to what is being said. She listens attentively and asks follow-up questions to explore what is being said to her. When a leader is genuinely listening to her team members, she pays attention to non-verbal cues such as body language, mood, facial expression and changes in behavior whether it is typical or out of character.

When leaders do not listen to their teams, they never get to know what their team members are really thinking about. Leaders must take time to have one-on-one meetings with team members to get more insight into what their team members are thinking about the tasks at hand and to understand what makes their team members tick. In these one-on-one meetings, leaders can also get to know when members are experiencing challenges with the task or even at home. Knowing what is on your team member's mind will help you as a leader to be more compassionate and provide suitable support to your team members.

Leaders must be confident and work with people who are most likely to give honest feedback. Leaders must be secure enough in their leadership roles to be able to accept this feedback. It is not uncommon to find leaders who prefer their own ideas above those of their team members.

Case Study

In a certain workplace, the team leader always struggled to take any inputs from the team members. The leader also used public humiliation and public ridicule to deal with team members. Team members became more and more withdrawn and many of them could be heard talking ill of the Team Leader and losing respect for the team leader. A very toxic environment was created in a very short space of time. The end result of this experience was a total rebellion of the team members.

Listening to the team is an ongoing and very important task. One practice that assists the listening process is also having occasional culture surveys to check if as a leader one is still upholding the culture of listening and walking in tandem with one's team.

4.0 How to improve your listening skills

1. Forget your ego.

Everything is **not** about you. Really! Give a genuine ear to your team members and ask them about their lives.

2. You must be open to learn from your team members

The beauty of working with people is that every day is an opportunity to learn something new from them. Your team members are also your life- long educators.

3. Listen meaningfully to understand.

Many of us listen in order to respond, not to understand. Genuine listening has a built-in desire to understand and learn from someone.

4. Be interested.

When you are interested as a team leader, you will ask follow-up questions. You will incorporate the thinking you gleaned from a team member into your plan of action.

5. Give yourself enough time to listen

Do not rush people. Give them enough time to speak and for you to re- ally hear them. This means that you do not schedule one-on-one meetings when you are chasing deadlines.

6. No phone, tablet or laptop

You must give your team members your full attention. Give them the respect of focusing on them and what they are communicating to you.

7. You must care

Be genuinely interested and care about what the team members are communicating to you.

In this trade union setting, the team leader took plenty of time consulting the team members before taking any course of action. This re- ally built the team's trust in the team leader. Team members felt comfortable in approaching the team leader with any suggestions about developments within the space. Team members found the team leader always ready to listen to them. Even when the team leader chose a different course of action, team members were very satisfied, because feedback was given about why a different course of action was taken.

Chapter 6: Leading like a woman means you are also a servant leader

1. Introduction

Servant leadership is a leadership style in which the main goal and motivation of the leader is to serve. This is very different from traditional leadership where the leader's focus is poised on themselves as leaders, focused only on the success of their business, institution or organization. A person who is a servant leader considers the needs of the employees or team members or followers first. A servant leader pulls out all the stops to ensure that her team develops and performs as highly as possible. In servant leadership, the leader exists to serve the people.

When leaders shift their mindset and serve first, they are not the only beneficiaries of this mindset, but their employees also benefit. In servant leadership employees, team members and followers acquire personal benefits which can be personal growth for employees and team members or it can be access to benefits and the securing of their interests in the case of followers. Servant leadership protects the growth and impact of the organization, business or institution. This is aided by the employees' growing commitment and growing loyalty to the institution, organization or business. Since this leadership style came about, several different organizations have adopted this style as their way of leadership. This style of leadership contributes significantly to the success of businesses, organizations and institutions because the teams who work under these leaders have job satisfaction, commitment and loyalty and it tends to have a spill-over effect on the clients and followers.

Servant leadership as a leadership style and practice has been around for centuries as witnessed by the followers of this theory of servant leadership often quoting religious text and Jesus Christ, however, it was Greenleaf who developed the theory of servant leadership in the 20th century and who came to the realization that a leader should be someone that followers, team members can relate to. Hence Greenleaf's idea of what a Servant Leader should be. Greenleaf first developed his idea of Servant Leadership for use in an organizational sense while he was working as an executive at AT&T. Many other proponents/ supporters of servant leadership often refer to Jesus Christ as a servant leader by referring to what he said and what he did in for example the "washing of the disciples' feet".

Jesus Christ is seen as a leader who was committed to serving his disciples and seeing his disciples as equals. This "washing of the disciples' feet" not only portrayed that he wasn't afraid to be seen as equal in the eyes of his disciples, but it also shows that he prioritized his disciples first, as a servant leader should do, because foot washing was a job for servants not for "the Master" as Jesus was often referred to by his disciples. In Greenleaf's theory the emphasis of a servant leader is an "I serve" mentality as opposed to the traditional leadership "I lead" mentality. This signifies that a servant leader is an altruistic leader. She puts the interest of others above her interests. The leadership role emerges out of a strong desire to serve.

2.0 How to Become a Servant Leader

Servant leaders use a combination of these ten traits to lead:

1.0 Listening

2.0 Empathy.

3.0 Healing.

4.0 Awareness.

5.0 Persuasion.

6.0 Conceptualization.

7.0 Foresight.

8.0 Stewardship.

9.0 Commitment to the growth of people.

10. Building community.

In servant leadership, the priority of a leader is to serve. This demands of a leader to be a great listener. For servant leaders to be effective, they need to constantly improve their listening skills. They need to show respect and honor to their team members and/or followers.

Case Study

One of the most impressive qualities of Nelson Mandela, the first African President of post-democratic South Africa, was his ability to listen. In one of the meetings that he held with the Teachers' Union, SADTU, the President revealed this trait. The teachers were striking for better salaries and the salary negotiations had reached a dead-lock. In the meeting that he held with the union he really listened. He engaged with the National Office Bearers of SADTU. He asked questions. He challenged the leadership. The President displayed great listening skills. He displayed interest, humility and respect to the leadership of the union. It was clear that in the arsenal of leadership skills, he also had superb listening skills. After this meeting, the salaries of the teachers were improved. He also had the reciprocated respect of the leaders of the union.

Empathy

Servant leaders strive to go to the root of why people do the things they do, what motivates them, what their intentions are, to understand their ideas and their perspectives. Servant leaders have absolutely **no ego** as a result; it is very easy for them to set aside their personal viewpoints to look at things from the perspective of another team member or follower. They always approach situations with an open mind and not from the perspective of long- held beliefs. This is one of the reasons they are successful leaders.

Healing

Leading like a woman demands that a leader must genuinely care about the well-being of her team and of her people. Leading like a woman means that a leader cannot be faint-hearted. A leader **must** have a big heart that is strong enough to look at the emotional health and well-being of her immediate team members and the beneficiaries. Being a servant leader and leading like a woman means that you must tap into that pure and perfect spot with- in yourself to provide the best conditions within which people work or live or play or engage in their activities. The healing aspect of leading like a woman or being a servant leader means that when you undertake your leadership task, you must be able to have/ or co-ordinate the acquisition of knowledge, resources or support that people need to work or live or play or engage in their activities. In this context people are happy and engaged in their roles.

Self-Awareness

Self-awareness is a very important quality for a leader who is leading like a woman and for servant leaders to have. This is critical if you fall within the category of people who are undermined simply because they are women or simply because they are fat or simply because they are young or simply because they are black.

You must introspect your own motivations, emotions and behavior. If you are coming up with certain interventions purely to inflict revenge on someone, you need to stop that intervention and come up with an intervention that is building not destructive.

Leaders who lead like a woman, or servant leaders, are aware of their strengths and weaknesses, and do not feel any shame in asking for help. Leaders who have embraced servant leadership are great at handling their emotions and considering how these affect the people around them.

Case Study:

A certain leader in an NGO environment was misinformed about the character of a specific team member. Initially she was very suspicious of anything that this staff member did even how she sat in meetings. As time went by, she realized that she had been manipulated by one of her team members and began to see the great points about that team member. She was able to see that, that staff member was in fact a great member to have in her team as she did not need much supervision and always met her deadlines. She discovered that the team member who had spread malicious rumors was, in fact, the team member who had difficulty with sticking to her mandate.

In this scenario, the leader had not used her own lens to see all her team members. Being a self-aware leader, she was able to pick up that her expectations of the behavior of the maligned staff member were not being met. As a self-aware individual, the leader was able to adjust her view of her team and negotiated for the shifting of the rumor monger to another unit away from her department.

Persuasion/ Illustration

Servant leaders use persuasion or illustration or showing to get people to support their recommendations and decisions. They do not use their authority when they encourage people to act, implement programs and projects. Servant leaders use engagement, communication and consultation to get people to implement recommendations and decisions.

Visionary

Servant leaders and leaders who lead like a woman take time to review their institutions and organizations and to set a long-term vision and direction for their organizations or institutions. These are developed as a strategy for the organization's improvement and growth. Other leaders of units / departments take this strategy and use it to develop the department/ unit vision and mission that will support the overall strategy of the organization/ institution.

Foresight

Servant leaders have foresight or an advanced view of what may happen in the organization because of their actions because of experience. They also build these scenarios into how they build their organizations or institutions.

Leaders who lead like a woman, hopefully, have grown incrementally from the different levels of leadership as these help you to be able to have fore- sight and to prepare, in your mind, for different scenarios. Nonetheless all new leaders need to have mentors and/ or counsel to assist leaders to use the expertise and tools that are available to them to develop foresight and to be ready with suitable responses.

Case Study:

A servant leader in a church often emphasizes the issue of regular prayer and bible reading as a staple diet for all new members of the church. She indicates that people who do not pray and read their bible regularly are always asking for prayers from the leadership. She also predicts that those people who do not get into a prayer and bible reading regime almost always disappear from church.

The experience of the servant leader in this case study is that you can identify new converts who will grow in the church and those who will fall off. She also indicates that she has developed other mechanisms to provide support to new converts that is implemented by other leaders that she supervises in the church.

For your environment, you need to have foresight about how people may respond to the initiatives that you are introducing. You can consult with a suitable team of counselors or suitable service providers about the best course of action to minimize the impact of challenges that may come.

Stewardship

Stewardship is about taking responsibility. A servant leader is the one that is in the firing line in cases where her team underperforms or misses its tar- gets. A servant leader is the one who gets the congratulations when the team is doing particularly well.

It is true that most leaders have an idealized view of leadership as some- thing that will give you recognition, but in reality; leadership is a huge responsibility. This means that leaders have a responsibility of building or causing systems that work to be developed in their organizations or institutions. When systems work well, the institution can thrive. It also means that leaders must ensure that institutions continue to serve the purpose(s) for which they have been established.

Leaders who lead like a woman, servant leaders, formal leaders, informal leaders all have a responsibility for the things that happen in their organizations/ institutions. Leaders really must take the task of leadership seriously; look at their values in juxtaposition to organizational/ institutional values so that they can understand how they will support the company values in their leadership role. Servant leaders and leaders who lead like a woman must lead by example. They cannot expect certain behaviors from people when they fail to display those behaviors.

Commitment to the Development of People

Servant leaders, just like transformational leaders, are committed to the personal and professional development of everyone in their teams or amongst the followers.

Part of the work that leaders who lead like a woman or servant leaders undertake is the work of developing their teams and/ followers. To develop the capacity and the potential of your team, one needs to investigate/ research the professional development needs (and personal development needs) of the team members. This will help them to get to the level they need or want to be in their professional and personal lives.

Building Community/ Collegiality

The last characteristic is to do with building a sense of community or collegiality within your organization. Leaders who want to lead like a woman do this by providing opportunities for team members to interact with one another across the organization or institution. Other institutions and companies do this by holding annual gatherings for the entire team or monthly social events for the small team or branch for big organizations.

These can be in the form of lunches, dinners etc.

The organizational/ institutional spaces can also be organized to allow for informal gatherings of team members. This can also be built into meeting agendas where team members can chat about non-business aspects of their lives and share in team meetings.

Comparison of Servant leadership to Transformational Leadership

It is recommended that leaders use a combination of leadership styles. These leadership styles are comparable and where they are markedly different, certain situations may call for a vastly different style. In a toxic environment, one needs a variety of leadership styles including those styles that are deemed unpopular or tough leadership styles. The most important thing is that a leader must be educated about leadership, about their environment, and be confident. If one is still growing in one's role of leader- ship, it is advisable to use consultative and interactive styles of leadership. In toxic environments the leader needs to play the role of investigator/ re- searcher to understand the history of the environment, the organization/ institution one is leading. They also need to understand the role players and what motivates role player behaviors. Once a leader is clear about the factors at play, she should be decisive in dealing with the issues.

More on this in the next chapter.

Nevertheless, let us look at the comparisons of characteristics between servant leadership and transformational leadership

Transformational Leadership	Servant Leadership
Change people and systems Listening Visionary Charismatic Great communicators Supportive Self-multiplies Teambuilding Empathetic Develops people Role modeling/lead by example Consultative/ Collective decision-making Inspirational/Motivational Intellectually stimulates Seeks high impact Works with the willing	"I serve" instead of "I lead" Listening Visionary Self multiplies Team building Healing Role modeling/ Lead by example Develops people Empathetic Self-Aware Persuasive/ Illustrative Conceptualization Great communicators Has foresight Takes responsibility for team failures, builds whole community Emphasize beneficiaries/ focus on beneficiaries

There are many similarities between these two leadership styles except for a few differences namely: the premise for Servant Leadership is "I serve" in- stead of "I lead" and the fact that the transformational leader works with those who are willing. The major similarity between the two is that with both styles of leadership, team members exhibit high levels of job satisfaction.

Chapter 7: Leading Like a Woman is Tough

1. Introduction

Leading like a woman can be **tough**. What does this mean? It can be strong, it can stretch, it can respond appropriately to a difficult situation. Some- thing tough is resilient. Something tough must weather the storms and challenges. This ability to be tough needs to be distinct and different from being **hard.** Something hard can hurt or harm someone. Something hard can be harsh. Something hard can be threatening. Something hard is de- fined in this book as unfeeling, but for leaders who lead like a woman being tough means that this leader is not afraid to feel and is not afraid to be vulnerable.

2. Being tough and leading like a woman

In the space of authority and leadership, a leader will be subjected to tests of different kinds. The tests that one gets in leadership can be applied on a leader deliberately and consciously by some or all the team members. Some of the tests can emerge out of the real context, situation and conditions of the organization or institution. In all these, leaders must display a certain level of toughness.

It is quite common for women to be tested by their team members and/ or followers especially in environments that have been male spaces. Also, in spaces where leadership has been an area of the white race group, when the race of a leader changes, one may be subjected to tests.

Case Study

In another workplace context, a leader who happened to be the first African woman leader found herself tested in a few areas. When she was appointed, she learnt that at least one person did not expect her to last more than three months in that leadership role. What followed her appointment was a series of tests. In the first test, she had to deal with petty fights between members of staff. She handled these quite easily and after these, she found that one of the Departmental Managers did not appreciate taking instructions from her. After giving a warning to that Manager, this member of staff persisted in this behavior and the leader in this situation proceeded to charge this member of the Management corp. When a hearing was held, this Manager was dismissed.

In the case study above, the insubordination of the Manager needed to be dealt with speedily. Action was taken in the sixth month of the new woman leader and showed that the woman leader was willing to address the challenges that emerged within the organization.

The McKinsey & Company Report on Africa also indicates as quoted earlier that another success factors the women mentioned was the courage to dissent or take an unpopular line. Taking an unpopular line is also evidence of being tough. Leaders who lead like a woman cannot seek to be popular at the expense of organizational needs.

Case Study

In a particular environment the Chief Executive Officer, who was a woman, decided to resign when she realized that the line she had decided to take was unpopular with the Chairperson of the Board, who was a man.

In the case study above, we see that the CEO did not take the line that was suggested by the women in the cited McKinsey Report. Needless to say, the issues that were plaguing that particular environment continue to plague it till this day. In this case study we see the importance of being tough even if it means becoming unpopular, if being tough can lift an organization from a serious quagmire.

Chapter 8: Leading Like a Woman is Compassionate

1. Introduction

The world is crying out for compassionate leadership. Many of the people who rise and succeed in going into leadership do so by pulling themselves up by their bootstraps, struggle against odds to emerge as leaders. Those struggles are often very harsh and not conducive to developing compassion in leaders. Many of them are truly smart, highly intelligent, visionary, great planners; but are they compassionate human beings?

If you are alert and have lived on planet earth for more than eighteen years, you certainly can attest to the fact that not all leadership is compassionate. Just looking at the political leadership that we have had in the last 5 years across the globe; we can see some of the leadership that has had to be relieved of leadership because people felt that the leadership was not touched or moved by their plight and was ignoring and neglecting their needs. These cases, referred to in this paragraph, portray the opposite of compassionate leadership.

2. Defining Compassionate Leadership

Compassion is something that forms part of the qualities that we ascribe to decent human beings. Compassion is an integral part of the curriculum when one is socializing children or little human beings. Compassion is learnt and developed as part of the process of socialization. Different societies seek to breed this quality amongst their young; but the value of compassion is not equal across all global societies. A brief scan of different types of societies shows that advanced societies, except perhaps for the Scandinavian countries, do not place compassion very high in the list of qualities that human beings can have. Amongst developing societies, compassion is seen as an important value, even though this is changing, especially in urban centers.

Compassion is that quality that shows up as an inclination and a yearning to understand other people and be kind to them. Compassion is the ability to sympathize and empathize with other people. Compassion is the ability to 'feel with' and 'feel for' other people. Compassion means that you are self- aware and aware of the environment in which you operate. Compassion means you are interested in understanding the different circumstances of different people, because you care. Compassion means caring about people. It is the opposite of indifference or not caring. In the "ubuntu" framework discussed earlier, compassion is the interwoven, integral aspect of community interactions where we do not see ourselves as separate from each other but connected. In this frame, your pain is my pain, your joy is my joy.

Compassionate leaders display the above qualities by valuing their team members as an integral and significant part of the organization/ institution. Compassionate leaders seek to ensure that they build supportive, inclusive, healthy organizations/institutions. Part of the leadership effort is expended in ensuring the well-being and happiness of the team and/ or followers. Compassionate leadership is motivated about the meaningful interventions that support teams and/ followers over an extended period for the sustainability of an organization/ institution.

3. Compassionate leadership and gender

Compassion is often associated with women in most societies. This is the case because boys and girls are socialized differently. Girls are taught to take care of others whilst boys are taught to go for what they want. This differentiated socialization disadvantages boys in the compassion stakes. They also do not develop self-awareness about their own capacity, skills levels, competencies, strengths and weaknesses. The way in which they measure their strengths out of 10 is weaknesses= 0 and strengths=10. With that being said, not all boys and men are self-unaware, have low levels of compassion and completely devoid of skills for dealing with feelings and emotions. The change that needs to happen in all societies is that boys and men's compassion and emotional intelligence needs to be developed consciously and equally with that of girls and women.

Some experiences of women erode sympathy especially for other women e.g. women who have been abused can see other women as soft or fragile and needing to develop more resilience in dealing with patriarchy and thus less sympathetic to those who may be novices in dealing with the more toxic types of masculinity and patriarchy. It may also make them completely unsympathetic to men in general and see men as the devil.

4. Why is compassionate leadership important?

The time for compassionate leadership is now when people are crying out for compassionate leadership and compassionate eco-socio-political systems. The riots and protests across the globe are an indication that the world is crying out for compassionate leadership and systems. The systems that have thrived in the 20th century have been very alienating for people and we have attempted to change the leadership styles to be people-friendly, but we experienced a disjuncture because the systems themselves were not based on compassion and recognition of our connectedness as humanity.

As the paragraph above indicates, it is becoming more of a demand for leaders to be compassionate. Many people have the mistaken belief that displaying compassion is a sign of weakness. They could not be further from the truth. Compassion involves using the strongest muscle in the human body and that is the heart. It is the strongest muscle and it requires exercise just like other muscles to be strong. Caring for and about people even when conditions seem to militate against this is a sign of strength. Caring for people is not for weak and fragile hearts.

Compassionate leadership is not about tweaking your leadership retinue. I feel strongly that people who have no love for people in general should not lead, but alas, they are the most prevalent people you will find in leadership.

5. Characteristics of compassionate leaders

They are more engaging, and can create higher levels of overall employee engagement

They build robust, trusting relationships at all levels

They are viewed as being strong

They inspire greater collaboration within organizations

They contribute to lower rates of employee turnover

They inspire their people to feel more connected to one another

They create environments where employees feel a greater sense of commitment to

Source: https://www.emergenetics.com

1. Compassionate leaders have no ego

2. Compassionate leaders genuinely care about people

3. Compassionate leaders always find time to hear from other people and consider their inputs seriously

4. Compassionate leaders are accountable- they give regular feedback to individuals and groups

5. Compassionate leaders contribute visibly to the personal and professional development of their teams.

6. Compassionate leaders go the extra mile for their teams and/ followers their happiness, their benefits, their conditions.

. Compassionate Leadership in action

Very important for leaders who want to lead like a woman. What leaders can do to be more compassionate?

Be available

This means that leaders must be available for their teams. This can be in the form of regular individual meetings that are scheduled and diarised. When you are available, be present in that moment. Pay attention to what is being communicated, Take it seriously. Be respectful to your team members.

1. Be a lifelong learner

To be a compassionate leader, you must be open to learning new things. It does not matter how old you are, but you must still be able to learn from others, especially the young as they almost always have fresh new ideas of seeing, being, thinking and doing.

2. Stop your selfish ways/ Be unselfish/Be selfless

You must be able to show people that the things you do and the things you propose are for the benefit of all and not just for your benefit. What will help with this is consistency. One has to be consistent in leadership. The consistency for a woman leader is about: campaigning for women leadership and well-being, caring about the people in the organization/ institution, responsive to people in the organization/ institution, stand for people (organization/ institution) even under difficult conditions etc. Be able to take the heat on behalf of your team.

3. Be open to change

Possess the ability to see things from another person's perspective. Be able to change your thinking based on actively engaging with others. Be able to change your routine and your expectations to accommodate others. Be able to give more of yourself to accommodate others.

Chapter 9: Leading Like a Woman is Forgiving

1. Introduction

When human beings get together in groups in non-voluntary situations as in workplaces, where people come together for the main purpose of generating an income to sustain their livelihoods; there are many other factors that are at play. By this is meant that a range of factors come into focus e.g.:

- There are people who are "not morning people",

- There are people who have never learnt to be accountable and will not take responsibility for anything

- There are people who are completely not self-aware and have not got- ten to know themselves as yet and do not have the skills to get to know themselves

- There are people who are naïve about group dynamics and different workplace characters

- There are people who have positive attitudes and there are people who have negative attitudes

- There are people who have navigated through life by using one trick: charm or bullying or manipulation etc.

- There are people who have had experience of leadership in the past

- There are people who are introverted and those who are extroverted

- There are people who can learn (are teachable) and there are people who believe that they have learnt all there is to know (not teachable)

- There are people who come from conservative value systems and those who come from alternative value systems

- There are people who observe situations (hands-off) and there are people who solve (engage) situations

- There are people who conform to the status quo and there are people who seek to change the status quo

- There are people who are leaders, but are uneducated about leader- ship

- There are people (many) who have been wounded in various ways during the course of their lives

- There are people who love to tell tales and carry gossip to and from different and/or opposing directions

The list of the various role-players can go on and on beyond this one, but the illustration that is made through this list is that leaders need to prepare themselves for various characters when they take leadership position. It also means that leaders must themselves be self-aware and know the types of behaviors and values that they do not like. Leaders should be able to deal with a wider variety of people, be able to discourage behaviors and values that are counter-productive to the organization or institution that one is leading.

2. Leadership and forgiveness

We have already noted in this book that leadership goes hand-in-hand with compassion, and where it does not, it is time for the leadership to review themselves and their practice. It is very important for the leadership to review themselves using a variety of methods especially the methods of independent (therefore objective) institutions. This is very important in a climate where many of our leaders are still male and are completely alienated from themselves. I need to indicate here that this alienation comes first from socialization challenges, if we understand that socialization is ongoing, within a patriarchal system. Whilst women tend to be more self-aware, it is not true that all women are self-aware, so objective evaluation is important.

We unequivocally want our leadership to be compassionate, therefore, in that frame it also becomes a key attribute for leadership to be forgiving. Leaders who hold grudges end up as total failures.

Case Study

In a for-profit environment, the leader responded very badly when the employees asked for a representative union and raised issues which included the issue of short-term contracts. Whilst those discussions were going on, he began a process of dismissals that targeted those employees who had temporary contracts. Coupled with that dismissals campaign, he began a very toxic divide and rule and intimidation campaign which made it difficult for the union to organize as permanent employees were openly supporting management. The individuals who were the drivers of the unionization process failed to access the Board to raise their grievances, so they got frustrated and all re- signed, one of them resigned with immediate effect. The leader continued to use sex for favors such as his girlfriend who had been employed on a short-term contract was irregularly made permanent. He continued to be negligent with the handling of company funds until the company went bankrupt and the shareholders realized that the financial reports were fictitious and fired him and sold the company at a loss. After such a massive disaster, this leader was able to get a job in government.

In the case study above, we realize that the leader was a vindictive individual. He immediately introduced changes that would get rid of the employees who had raised their discontent over being temporarily employed for a long time. He also got rid of people that he was holding grudges against. He did not put the interests of his organization/ institution in the centre of his decision-making and caused a lot of pain for a lot of people because of his un- forgiving nature. This leader was unable to manage his own emotions and to put the interests of his organization above his own and he destroyed many lives. Forgiving people is a courageous action we institute when people have made a mistake as people will because they are human, not when they have spoken up for themselves as in the example above.

Leaders need to be forgiving as part of their suite of leadership attributes. The incomplete list of characters that leaders will meet in the workplace indicates that there is variety and diversity in the workplace and that diversity needs to be recognized by leadership and managed effectively by the leader- ship. In that diversity, not everyone will appeal equally to a leader. Some people will have habits, values, statements, ideas and thought processes that you will not like as a leader. The leader must be compassionate to her- self first and understand that she will make mistakes in the process of executing her leadership role. She must also separate habits, values, statements, ideas and thought processes that do not affect the effective running of the organization/institution from those that do. Those that have a negative impact must be addressed and after that we keep it moving, we do not continue to harbor ill-will against team members/ followers who may have emerged with those negatively impactful issues.

Forgiving leaders and leaders who lead like a woman are not afraid to ask for help that will contribute to making them better and ever-improving leaders. To forgive, leaders must tap into skills and competencies that they may not immediately have. Going for help may be in the form of using mentors or in the form of accessing psychotherapy or counseling services. These interventions help leaders to view things from a different perspective and to emerge with alternative problem-solving skills. Using such interventions helps leaders to develop their emotional intelligence and makes them more effective leaders in a world that is crying out for compassionate and affirming leadership.

Part of a forgiving leadership is about the ability to forgive oneself when one has made a mistake, because leaders are human too and making mistakes is part of being human. Great leaders always forgive and find it easier to for- give others than it is to forgive themselves. Great leaders have more compassion for other people than they have for themselves. They are always ready to forgive others and to build peace between warring parties, but they hardly spare a thought for themselves. Therefore, it is important for leaders to be assisted or taught to build that compassion for themselves as it helps them to:

- Bounce back from a mistake much quicker

- Helps them maintain a balanced perspective and a sense of reality about the mistake

- Helps them to learn the do's and don'ts of leadership

- Helps them to have lower levels of anxiety about mistakes they are bound to make

- Helps leaders to focus on the future more instead of being obsessed by mistakes of the past

3. Forgiving leaders in action

Many people in the world always cast their mind back to the South African transition when they think about forgiving leadership. Two names always come up and those names are President Nelson Mandela and Bishop Desmond Tutu. I highly recommend the books written by both leaders to understand the humanity, compassion and 'ubuntu' that is the core of the two individuals.

In addition to the above, women have been the champions in forgiving people. If you have any meaningful experience of being human, you will know that women are professionals at the business of forgiving. In their personal lives they almost always must forgive a parent or an intimate partner and do not expect the impossible from the people in the teams that they lead hence the ability to forgive.

It is a real pity that women are often overlooked in leadership, because this means the few women that are in leadership must face many unnecessary challenges namely:

- Dearth of knowledge. We are not building enough knowledge about alternative leadership theory and practice since most leaders in the private and public sectors in the world are men.

- Society could be doomed to aeons of leadership that lacks self- awareness, is aggressive, prejudiced, testosterone-fuelled, manipulative, divisive, cowardly, unaccountable, exploitative, exclusionary, alienating and swaddled in toxic masculinity for the rest of the existence of this planet or the human life on this planet, with a few notable exceptions.

- The few women leaders may find it an uphill struggle to emerge with more humane and inclusive leadership styles and may remain trapped in practices that do not expose the slightly hidden gem that is woman leadership which is more nurturing, is more responsive to people's needs, has more compassion, has more courage, has more accountability.

Chapter 10: Leading Like a Woman in the Economy

1. Introduction

The economic space has been an interesting space that has evolved and continues to evolve over time. It has not always been the same in every geo- graphic location. In some spaces it was the preserve of men whilst in some spaces, women's virtue incorporated being an industrious, productive role player in the economy. In other spaces, women were actively kept out of the economy and kept in the kitchen and/or the hearth. In other spaces, class was a key determinant in whether one woman could be kept in the household. For poor women, the conditions dictated that one had to be a serf or a peasant or a domestic helper or one of the workers in the factory line. At the same time, women who were born of means and women who were married to men of means had to be kept indoors and/or moved amongst circles of means.

Africa is interesting because everybody worked in the business of sustaining life in pre-colonial times. Men and women worked on food production or food security, men and women worked on arts and crafts and other activities that sustained life. Older women looked after the very young children. The socialization space involved both women and men as education involved dividing children into different age groups and grouped on gender lines.

2. Women in the Economy

The global economy and the practices within the economy have been changing, particularly in the last 100 years. Many of the changes were precipitated by the growth of technology in the last 50 years. The growth of technology allowed mass production and huge profits for businesses. The changes have not prioritized justice for women in the economy.

Patriarchy remains very rife in the economy, regardless of the sector in which men and women work. This has affected mostly women in the economy in the following way:

- Leadership of companies at Board (Governance level) and at CEO (Executive and/or Management level) has remained a male sphere despite the McKinsey Reports that indicate that organizations that are led by women or who have women at the top perform better on a few performance indicators, including the profit indicator.

- Women are the most vulnerable to the experience of gender-based violence (GBV) and sexual harassment in the workplaces. This means that others such as men and gender non-conforming individuals do experience these social ills in their workplaces, but it is not comparable to the levels that women experience these ills. Many victims of sexual harassment report a negative impact to their health when these incidents of sexual harassment are not quickly resolved. Many women report that they had to quit their jobs without an alternative or seek alternative employment because of an unbearable situation of sexual harassment that was not dealt with in their workplace. Many women report that employers either resist or find it difficult to deal with re- ported incidents of sexual harassment.

- The global economy has found it difficult or has resisted the presence of women in the economy. This is revealed in the unequal salaries that women earn in the economy for the same positions that men hold. It is very common for a woman who is a legal expert/ accountant in a company to earn less than her male counterpart. This has been on the agenda to be changed for decades now, but it still has not changed completely.

- The global economy has found it difficult or is actively resisting the presence of women because women's conditions of service and benefits are still contested. This is revealed in the uneven and widely varied maternity benefits across the globe. In some countries, read Scandinavian countries paid maternity leave can be as much as two years whilst in some countries women only get two months off and in other countries those months taken as maternity leave are not paid by the company, women take them at their own risk, and in others only a portion of a woman's salary is paid and it's a toss of a dice who will pay between government and the employer.

- Women's issues are not always addressed. They are usually swept under the carpet. They are often used to keep women out of the formal economy or to justify why women's numbers are lower in the formal economy.

- Trade union representatives, leaders and collective bargaining representatives are often male and where women are included, they are of- ten there as tokens of woman representation. The issues that women want to bring to the collective bargaining table are often not under- stood by the mostly male leadership and bargaining team. These is- sues are the first to fall off the table when it is time for bargaining and prioritization of workers' demands.

- Employers benefit from patriarchy because they can pay lower salaries to women and they can get away with being irresponsible corporate citizens who do not acknowledge the pressures that women go under as mothers, care-givers and employees.

- The unjust economy accounts for why most women are poorer after retirement, because their salaries are always low, and they cannot save enough for retirement. At the same time women are recorded as the highest investors in the education of their children and they are the ones who spend the most on the care of the young and old in their extended families.

- The structure of the global economy perpetuates women's junior role in the economy as banks are not always keen to fund women's start- ups. This has the effect that big businesses and multi-nationals are owned by individual men or groups of men. Women mostly operate in the SMME category of business. "The Global Entrepreneurship Monitor (GEM) Report for Women 2016/17 reports that 274 million women were already running their own businesses across 74 economies, of which 111 million were running well-established businesses by 2016. Women are known to give back about 90 percent of their earnings to the health and education of their communities and families, contributing to development directly, so it's easy to see why it is critical." www.entrepreneur.com.

It is not yet clear how women are taking advantage of global trade agreements for the benefit of their businesses. This is an area on which information is needed. If one generalizes the footprint of patriarchy to this, it becomes clear that this is an area in which progressive collectives need to transform, for the benefit of women.

3. Leading like a woman in the Economy

Leadership in the economy needs to change. The exclusionary and greedy practices that thrive in today's economy need to be eradicated or at the very least reduced. The "Fourth Industrial Revolution" must be tampered by a people-centered approach, if we are to improve economic conditions of billions of people. Towards the end of the 20th century-to date, the middle class and its fortunes have declined, and the economic benefits of labor have become increasingly monopolized by the top layer of economic leadership. At the same time, women have dominated the lowest rungs of the economy. The following paragraphs begin to prick what could be integrated into the "leading like a woman in the Economy" arsenal.

Responsible Corporate Citizenship

The leadership that is desirable, therefore, will be a leadership that promotes responsible corporate citizenship. Responsible corporate citizenship is not solely focused on the generation of profit to the exclusion of all else.

Corporate citizenship concerns itself also with how it affects the surrounding communities and the environment. Leading like a woman in building responsible corporate citizenship seeks to make a difference in the surrounding communities and to have a positive impact on the environment. This means that CEOs must have an appreciation for investing their social responsibility funds in NGOs that benefit women and children. This means that the company must assess the development impact it seeks amongst the communities it operates in and to develop its programs in consultation with the intended beneficiaries.

It also cannot just throw money at an issue, but it needs to be involved and respectful. CEOs cannot hope that junior employees in the Social Responsibility Unit of the company will do the work. The participation of the executive leadership displays the company's commitment to this. The plans of the company to reduce its carbon footprint, to rehabilitate the environment must also not be done haphazardly but they must be geared at having a maximum impact. CEOs of companies who lead like a woman should not be disputing points on responses to the climate change challenge.

The Owners and Managers of Enterprises

In most companies globally, with a few exceptions, the profit is not distributed fairly between the owners and managers on the one side and the employees on the other side. Leaders who lead like a woman need to start incorporating self-control to the rabid greed that characterizes companies today. This means that there should be standards that companies set to reward talent and commitment from the bottom to the top. It means that there must be recognition that the generation of profit is a collective effort and wages and salaries must be able to reflect this and be able to regulate and control the wage-gap that exists between the highest earner and the lowest earner in a company.

Companies who are led by leaders who lead like a woman must create work- ing environments that are inclusive and where all workers feel safe. That means that issues of bullying and sexual harassment in the workplace must be prevented through the development of comprehensive policies, ongoing education and awareness-raising about unpalatable behaviors in the con- text of the workplace as well as consistent implementation of those policies. This means that companies must provide employee wellness programs that are cognizant that workers and managers come from different socializing contexts and some of those contexts do not promote peace and mutual respect in a workplace and work towards re-socializing workers and managers towards the culture that is desired in that workplace.

Leaders who lead like a woman in the economy must eliminate any discriminatory practices from their workplaces and these may affect migrant workers, gender non-conforming workers, disabled workers, young workers and women workers. They must evaluate their policy and their practice by making use of independent and objective service providers the better to improve their environments. These may be difficult sessions, but leaders will be glad they undertook such initiatives.

These groups of workers namely: migrant workers, gender non-conforming workers, disabled workers, young workers and women workers may need certain measures of support that respond to their situations and owners and managers need to be awake as to what those needs may be and how best to address them in the company. Leaders who lead like a woman need to be responsive to these needs and to be supportive of all their employees.

Case Study

In a multi-national company which was based in South Africa, one South African woman lost her mother. In the South African context, the legislation only gives five days per year for family responsibility and there is no extra allocation of days for bereavement. This young African lady applied for leave to go and bury her mother who was buried quickly. She stayed away from work for three working days. On the following Monday, whilst she was really getting to grips with her mother's passing her leader, a woman, called and demanded that she get back to work. When another team member, shortly after that, lost her mother she was given a month off and was called regularly by the leader to be reassured and told to take all the time she needed. The latter lady was white.

This case study shows inconsistency, discrimination, favoritism and lack of self-awareness. In the case study above two of the people were European and one was African, and the African woman was not treated as a human. Her grief was not understood by her European leader and, for obvious reasons, this generated grave resentment as the African lady felt very aggrieved and she felt that she was without recourse in that environment.

Trade Unions and Employee Representatives

This group of role players in the economy needs to address several things to integrate ethos of 'leading like a woman' namely:

- Decisively deal with patriarchy in their structures and in their work- places. This means that they need to learn and educate each other about patriarchy and how it affects women and men. It means they must be self-critical and critical of each other using a gender lens to evaluate themselves on the question of patriarchy and the eradication of patriarchy. Build their consciousness on alternatives to patriarchy.

- Promote woman leadership (in the trade union, in the workplace and in society) and support consciousness building on a range of issues including the eradication of patriarchy and the implementation of progressive alternatives to patriarchy and interventions that promote substantive and meaningful gender equality.

- Address the sexual division of labor at work and at home. Under- stand that women do a lion's share of the reproductive work and still must partake in productive work and work towards an equitable share of work at home and in the workplace. Increasing men's role in reproductive labor is an important aspect of transformation as we move forward.

- Address issues of the gender gap in salaries. Trade unions have yet to raise this issue across all sectors seriously let alone addressing it decisively. The issue persists because it is not an area that trade unions have tackled consistently and across all sectors in the economy.

- Address issues of violence, GBV, harassment and sexual harassment in the world of work (and in society). Trade unions are already organized, they should be able to port the campaigns they have in the work space to the community space. Leading like a woman involves transforming lives of workers and people for the better.

Legislators, Policy- Makers and Influencers in the Economy

Legislators and policy-makers are found at a global level in multilateral institutions and in nations. The role of these legislators and policy makers is very crucial as their decisions do affect billions of people at grassroot level. They need to be conscious of how their decisions impact on the people who often pay the price with their lives and with the quality of their lives because of decisions made at these lofty levels.

Influencers are individuals and collective structures of interest groups such as trade unions, NGOs, communities and businesses. These structures of- ten have the opportunity, if not the equal capacity, to influence the decisions of legislators and policy makers in the economy.

All these role-players need to integrate the following thinking into their decision-making processes:

- Re-imagining reproductive labor. By this is meant a conscious move and effort in valuing the contribution of reproductive labor into the GDP of the various nations. This may involve some thinking about how different family units are supported in providing this reproductive labor. All the role-players can put on their thinking caps in emerging with proposals that have to be subjected to consultation, considering the differences in different nations and within different nations to emerge with relevant and responsive measures of valuing and sup- porting reproductive labor. This can assist in the reduction of socio- economic inequalities, if implemented.

- Increasing the participation of women and other disadvantaged communities in the making of decisions about legislation and policy at global and national level.

- Increasing the capacity of role-players and beneficiaries in decision- making processes about economic legislation and policy at all levels. This is critical as many beneficiaries are often called to support initiatives that militate against their interests.

- Integrate mainstreaming of gender and of disability to ensure that decisions taken at these forums do not discriminate against anyone or even achieve unintended results for some communities.

- Focus on the reduction of inequalities in our societies that allow for conditions of enslavement of some sections of humanity all over the world.

Chapter 11: Leading Like a Woman in Political Spaces

1. Introduction

Some research about the early communal societies where everyone's labor and contribution were valued as it was understood in the context of survival of a village. It is only with the rise of feudalism and the industrial revolution that the differences between wealthy men and poor men as well as between men and women became more clearly marked because of the changing material conditions that allowed others to usurp and monopolize common goods like land and water as well as people. In these arrangements we saw the emergence of classes and unequal gender relations.

At the beginning of the organization of society along political lines strong men rose to leadership as a direct consequence of their ability to monopolize common goods for themselves and to organize others to fight to protect that monopoly. History shows that this happened in various ways in different societies, but the long and the short of it is that this was developed into a sys- tem of beliefs one of which was it is natural for a family to spawn kings. The dynamics of contestation of this concept have led us to the situation we have today where some countries have recognized royalty alongside a 'democratic' system of elected political leadership; whilst other countries have completely eradicated the idea of royalty. The changes in the political landscape have also seen a series of revolutions and uprisings across the globe that resulted in reformulation of borders and a reformulation of political governance structures. Whilst all this has been going on, women were not included as participants, except as caterers and servants of the great men.

"We are told that the first country to give a *conditional vote* to women was Sweden between 1718 and 1771 and that some women in the Isle of Mann (part of the British Isles) gave some women *the right to vote* in 1881. In 1906 Finland became the first country in the world to give universal suffrage (1- man 1 vote). The first women parliamentarians were elected in Finland in 1907. In 1853 Velez province in New Granada colony (now Colombia) gave universal suffrage to men and women but the **Supreme Court later** re- versed this provision for women." Zingiswa Losi, COSATU President in one of her inputs in 2018.

This history also indicates that political parties started as men's organizations and only later, in the 20th century, did they begin to include women. The cultures and ethos of political parties remains male-centric and patriarchal even where women are active members in those parties. It would be interesting to learn how political parties that have been formed by women in the latter part of the 20th century to date have fared in this regard, noting that women political parties are relative newcomers to the political space.

2. Women in Political Spaces

The participation of women in political spaces has been only marginally bet- ter than the participation of women in economic spaces. This is particularly true in the developing world where women's parliamentary participation has been significantly higher than their participation in economic spaces.

In the developing world women's economic participation is higher in the in- formal economy than it is in the formal economy. Also, women's participation in the formal economy is mostly in the lower rungs of the formal economy whereas in politics they tend to be very visible at national, state/ province and at local government levels. They are also visible in the leadership of political parties as well. They have even been visible as elected/ appointed Presidents or Prime Ministers or Acting Presidents for a short while.

In the developed world women have also been visible in politics especially as members of parliaments, party whips and speakers of parliament. Only a few developed countries have promoted women to position of President most notably Germany, United Kingdom, Norway, Ireland, France (for a year), Switzerland, New Zealand, Iceland, Australia and Denmark.

What is clear is that visible changes to women's lives have been clearer in the Scandinavian countries with some patchy impact in some developing countries in the case of supporting poor women develop their micro-enterprises, access to education, improved sanitation and clean water infra- structure, poverty relief programs and social grants. There is still a need to push for 50% and above leadership of women in political spaces the better to measure the impact of woman leadership in politics.

In many countries women's priorities must contend with typically male priorities that sometimes emerge as vanity projects such as the Gautrain project in Gauteng, South Africa. Other male priorities can be something such as The Wall on the border of Mexico and the United States and new cars each term for Executive Members of government.

Woman leadership must have a different focus. It cannot be bogged down by benefits to individual members of political leadership, but it must be seized with how the fiscus benefits the needy and vulnerable people in a society many of whom will be women and their children in the foreseeable future. It must be seized with how the lives of the neediest people are improved and not how those who can afford luxuries can be helped to reduce/ even avoid paying taxes.

Leadership in Political Spaces

There needs to be a shift in how leadership is done in political spaces. As communities, we must promote women and support them in the roles in which we have promoted them. Political structures must have at least 50% in leadership.

From political leaders the citizenry expects a lot because it pays taxes. There needs to be conversations held across nations about how the taxes are used to improve people's living conditions at home, before we spend on overseas priorities. Many countries continue to have very high Defense budgets even when they are not war mongers. Rich citizens cannot only be concerned about their interests, mostly because the have-nots (who also pay tax) can- not be expected to be patient forever whilst their interests are ignored by politicians in their quest to satisfy the rich and elite sectors of the population.

Leaders who lead like a woman use consultative methods of leadership to ensure that there is an interactive space between leaders and the population. In many countries, there is no space provided for citizens' inputs or the little space that is opened to hear from the citizens does not benefit the citizens as this is done for show and not from any real commitment to hear and act on the things that citizens are hoping for.

Leaders who lead like a woman also set aside funds for building citizen's capacity for effective engagement with democratic processes. It is useless to ask people to make inputs into processes they know nothing about and where they fear making inputs because they see this as a waste of their time because no-one will take their proposals seriously and implement them. Leaders who lead like a woman need to be transparent about what can be implemented and why not all proposals can be implemented instead of just set- ting priorities without giving feedback to the citizens. There is a lot of evidence that shows that citizen participation leads to more accountability from citizens and political leaders alike. People are more willing to pay tax if their views are taken on board and they receive regular and good information about government programs. Leaders who lead like a woman spend time and money on regular communication and feedback and engage with com- munities regularly and meaningfully, not only during election time and not only to talk without hearing from the citizens.

3. *Political Spaces and Gender Budgeting*

Gender budgeting becomes an important tool for leaders who lead like a woman. With gender budgeting, leaders can ensure that the government budget is used to address inequalities emanating from socio-economic inequalities. As women tend to be excluded from the mainstream economy, especially in developing countries; gender budgeting enables the state at various levels to pay a social wage that benefits the poor, a majority of whom are women. This allows the state to emerge with fiscal policies and spending measures that mitigate the effects of socio-economic inequalities for women and their offspring. In gender budgeting leaders consciously set targets that lift women out of abject poverty and to ensure that public funds are used strategically to ameliorate impacts of poverty, the burden of care work and poor access to infrastructure and services faced by the poor, the majority of whom are women.

4. Election of Party Office Bearers

Political parties ought to have capacity for research to be able to understand the factors that perpetuate gender inequality and patriarchy in the spaces in which they operate. That information must be disseminated widely within the political party for information sharing, discussion and to inform any policy review that may be necessary within the party to improve woman representation, empower women and transform political organizations into safe spaces for women and other marginalized groups. In Africa, some political parties have adopted a range of policies that accommodate women representation in political parties, amongst a range of other interventions. The issue that has not yet been dealt with in the African context is the issue of eliminating violence or the threat of violence completely from the process of electing new office bearers.

5. Post-national (provincial or municipal) elections

Any leader can lead like a woman, if they care sufficiently for all their citizens. Once a leader has won the elections, they need to address the needs of all the citizens. This has been severely challenged by powerful interests in- country and at global level. Leading like a woman means that leaders must be responsive to the needs of their citizens. The gender dynamics in modern society are such that the neediest citizens would most likely be women, globally speaking. This calls on decision makers to mainstream gender into their policies and plans, starting with ensuring that there is adequate political will for improving the conditions of the neediest citizens and that there are adequate skills for developing, implementing and monitoring policy (and gender mainstreaming) within their management structures. There should be ongoing consciousness raising of government leaders about policy choices and ensuring that issues affecting women and gender mainstreaming do not fall off the table.

Chapter 12: Leading like a woman in Public Security spaces

1. Introduction

Public security remains one of the most male-dominated spaces within the public services, next to public finance. In OECD countries, the data indicates that women employed in the public service are 58,2 % ranging from 70% where it is highest, in Sweden to 42% where it is lowest, in Japan. This is very different when one compares these figures to women in the police services globally. The data available globally indicates that the average representation of women in the police service is only 15, 4%. It is no wonder then that women continue to face an uphill struggle in the police service and in accessing police services as citizens and members of communities. The data on average representation of women in the military is
10, 75% with the highest being 40% in North Korea and the lowest being 0,6% in Pakistan, where data was available. This, probably, has an impact on the role of women and benefits of women in peacekeeping missions if one considers that active soldiers are often the ones playing a role in peacekeeping missions and very few civilians put their hands up to become part of peacekeeping missions.

2. The role of women in Public Security

The Police Service

Police women experience discrimination in terms of promotions, more sexual harassment than male counterparts, and record higher levels of job dissatisfaction, stress and health challenges.

Many women relate stories of favoritism when it comes to the issue of pro- motions. In some cases, women indicate that there are no real procedures that are used in promotions, but there is evidence of change in the police service where there are policies and procedures that inform how promotions can be accessed and selections made. This, however, does not completely remove perceptions of discrimination when officers are promoted. Women feel that they are sometimes diverted to specialized policing corps which removes them from competing for promotion posts. In some countries e.g. Estonia and South Africa, gender equality has become part of the policies of the police service and this does improve the position of women in the police service, but it does not address the issue of transformation of the cultural environment and the eradication of exclusionary patriarchal beliefs and practices. The improvements may be visible in increased presence of women in leadership, but not in building inclusive cultures within the police services.

The different policing styles of men and women have come up for discussion. In the United States, for example, it is believed that women's different policing styles are in fact good for the policing profession and for communities because policewomen tend to be less aggressive than their male counter- parts and are the least likely to go for the gun before any other policing tactic. In fact, the cases of excessive police brutality have pointed at policemen as perpetrators. The evidence also suggests that women have been very effective in dealing with children (where crimes affected children), women (where they were victims of crime) and youth (where they became susceptible to youth sub-cultures of crime and gangsterism).

Sexual harassment is a factor in the police service and women are some- times seen as sex objects and tools. Many policewomen do not find it easy to report cases of sexual harassment because of fear of secondary victimization as well as not being able (comfortable) to express themselves on sexual harassment. This is brought about by male cultures that trivialize sexual harassment and sexual assaults that can include use of social media, videos, unwarranted and unwelcome touching and so on. Women continue to be a minority in the police services across the world making it an uphill struggle to influence exclusionary male cultures within these police services.

This definitely impacts on how women experience policing and the police service. In South Africa, for example, which has the highest rates of GBV globally; women have also experienced rape from policemen during raids, at roadblocks and in detention. In addition, they do not get due support when they report GBV crimes committed against them or their children. In South Africa, the situation is prevalent that even policewomen are not always supportive towards women who have experienced GBV. This is an area that police services really must address, as it stems from the male-centric and patriarchal ways of seeing, thinking and doing. This suggests that in cases where the environment is dominated by toxic male cultures and patriarchy, even women are more insensitive to women's (and vulnerable groups') is- sues. The rate of femicide in South Africa of 18 out of 100 000 women killed in 2018 is too high, in fact the highest in the world. It indicates the level of uncurbed misogyny in the South African context, where the police often seem uncaring or uninformed about GBV patterns if one looks at the lacklustre response to incidents of intimate partner violence. Even the excessively high rates of HIV and AIDS in South Africa can partially be attributed to high levels of GBV where women are afraid to demand protection and at worst where they are raped and do not consent to sex.

The Military

As a minority in the army, women in military service find themselves experiencing some peer pressure to participate in the social activities that men in the army participate in. It is not difficult to understand why women would choose to participate in strip clubs considering the social nature of humanity. It is possible that women use these platforms that need to be problematical, analyzed and understood for what they are; to build collegiality with their male counterparts.

Women continue to be a minority in the global military suggesting that women's concerns and women's conditions may not be at the top in the list of military priorities. Women in the military do feel undermined as people who are tolerated and accommodated, but not really adding any value in the army. This shows up in how their views on strategy and tactics are not sought out nor expected. The army **has** opened to include women; however, it is not ready to include them as genuine equals. Women in the army some- times feel as if they are not heard. Women in the military say that they feel that they are in a never-ending test where they must consistently prove themselves to their male colleagues.

Single women in the military struggle with how they are perceived by both men and women. They struggle to establish relationships with men because of the role they play of defense and protection of civilians and perceptions of what an acceptable, comfortable role for women should be. Being a single woman in the military ends up being a lonely business. In addition, wives of male soldiers may be suspicious of single women soldiers, making life lonely and hard for single women soldiers.

Noting the ever-present threat of sexual harassment and sexual assaults that women experience in all spaces, with very few and thus negligible exceptions, the army is also another area where women are subjected to sexual harassment and sexual assaults. Whilst figures of 20-25% have been advanced as figures of women who experience sexual assaults or harassment in the army; it is quite possible that these figures relate only to reported cases. It is quite common for soldiers to tolerate hardships and if the mentality of a soldier is to toughen up, this probably means that women soldiers will not always report cases of sexual harassment and assault and choose to deal with them individually. Nonetheless, some women soldiers live in constant fear of being sexually assaulted.

In addition, women soldiers find that most of the protective gear and health facilities in the military do not accommodate them. Some women have had serious health problems resulting in lasting reproductive health problems because the medics in the military are not as au fait about women's health needs and tend to dismiss their health complaints. At play in such cases is the prevalent trivialization of women and their issues as well as the inability of male army doctors to realize when they are out of their depth. In such cases patriarchy has cost some women their lives when they can no longer reproduce because of critical misdiagnoses and botched surgeries.

The military as a traditionally male space continues to be discriminatory, to negate and to be biased against women, but the gender bias does not end in the military. Women ex-combatants continue to experience this gender bias even in civilian life where their sacrifices and contributions to the defense and protection of citizens are not acknowledged.

Peacekeeping Forces

There is an emerging narrative that gender issues are not adequately ad- dressed during the preparation of peacekeepers and so women deployed to peacekeeping missions are not always aware what the security issues of women peacekeepers are. They also may not be aware of what the gender power relations are in the communities to which they are deployed. The training of peace keepers has been identified as gender-neutral and not assisting in understanding the cultural and gender dynamics in the communities of deployment.

The South African contingent of peacekeepers felt that citizens in peace- keeping missions were more willing to trust men as they felt that there has not been a long enough experience with women as peacekeepers to judge and trust women in the role of peace keepers.

Women peace keepers were discriminated against based on lack of physical strength, they were discriminated psychologically and emotionally because of extreme forms of sexual violence against women in the peace keeping environments. They were discriminated again as they were viewed as an extra-security risk because of their gender and vulnerability to sexual violence in toxic male environments.

Women peacekeepers who served in positions of authority were not taken seriously, nor any respect afforded to them, they were ignored and subjected to sexual harassment aimed at denigrating them and there was no punitive action taken for sexual harassment.

There is an uncomfortable duality that exists in the South African military because it professes gender equality, but in peace keeping missions, women experience a gender bias and a constant threat of sexual assault.

3. Leading like a woman in Public Security

The Police Service

Leading like a woman in the police services involves a range of interventions that start with a paradigm-shift. This paradigm shift involves the use of gender mainstreaming within the police services.

Gender mainstreaming in community safety can be a transformative approach whose agenda is transformation of society. ''Gender equality in policing is not only a matter of representation of women in the police, but it is about different security needs of women and men, too. Thus, gender analysis of specific security needs of women and men is necessary for improving police work.'' according to Sonja Stojanovic Gajic of the Belgrade Centre for Security Policy. This means that there should be Education, Training and Development (ETD) on gender mainstreaming for all in the police services especially the leadership. There should be an increased number of women and other under-represented (e.g. LGBTI) groups in the leadership of the police service (analyzing and addressing barriers to promotion of women and other under-represented groups should be undertaken).

There should be a gendered analysis of the different security needs of men and women (women trafficking for sexual exploitation, harmful traditional practices, femicide or killing of women by intimate partners and male family members) Robbery, Gender Based Violence, Sexual Harassment, Stalking, Extortion, Homicide, Internet and Social Media Crimes. This gendered analysis will help improve the efficacy (efficiency and effectiveness) of the police. There is a need to con- duct a gendered review of policies and procedures to ensure equitable implementation by individual officers i.e. they are clear and easy to implement e.g. sexual harassment policy and promotions policy of the police services. There is a need to develop responsive policing that looks at the needs of women and men and other vulnerable and/ or discriminated groups (e.g. LGBTI. There is a need to identify areas where women are particularly vulnerable to crime and sharing this with the communities for awareness raising and prevention purposes.

When dealing with GBV, the following issues need to be considered:

- o prevention through partnerships and community engagement,

- o effective investigation to close any loopholes for convictions,

- o refuse to participate in corrupt practices which often lead to GBV perpetrators going free,

- o collaboration with justice to ensure more meaningful sentences for perpetrators of GBV

- o collection and simplification of GBV statistics for easier tracking

The police services have evolved from male-only spaces. In the 20th century, the policing profession has grown to include women and other genders. This means that it is still an area of challenge for the police services. For all genders to experience policing in a fair and just way, ongoing ETD must be undertaken by various police service institutions. Discriminatory, exclusionary and marginalizing beliefs and practices must be eliminated from services meant to benefit the public.

The Military

The military needs to integrate women into its ranks not to negate them and call on them to become faux men. The military must change to accommodate women just as a range of societal institutions have had to change to accommodate women.

Part of the change is the paradigm shift that will remove male-centered approaches to policies, uniforms, equipment, facilities and services for military personnel. Women's experiences in the military indicate that the environment is very hostile to women from the inability to deal with a virulent GBV culture in the military, discrimination and harassment of women even the inability of the medical corps within the military to provide effective services to women soldiers.

Leading like a woman in the military means that we affirm women, we accommodate women and we ensure that policies, uniforms, equipment, facilities and services can be used or accessed fairly by women soldiers as well. Leading like a woman in the military means that we remove the gender blinders that make it difficult to see leadership potential in a woman soldier and that we promote and support women soldiers. Leading like a woman in the military means that we pull out all the stops in ensuring that women, men and others do not experience GBV in the military corps.

Peacekeeping Forces

There is an urgency to engender the training received by peace keeping personnel as they prepare for deployment to peacekeeping missions. The training needs to look at the culture, language and gender the better to prepare the peace keeping forces. The training also needs to emphasize the principles of gender equality amongst the peace keeping personnel themselves. The training must also integrate case studies of why certain peace keeping missions worked and why others did not work so that would-be peacekeepers can be better prepared for the environments that they are going into.

It is important to implement R1325 and other relevant recommendations in peacekeeping efforts and in involving women in post conflict reconstruction; however, this means that foundational work needs to be done in the military about transforming the military and the peacekeeping forces. There is a need to eradicate patriarchal beliefs and practices that seek to negate women and women attributes in the army and the peace keeping forces. Women can play a meaningful role in the army without adopting male traits, mannerisms and thinking patterns.

There should be a space for women traits, mannerisms and thinking patterns. This means that we need to re-think the gender-neutral approach to army and peacekeeping training. How do we integrate gendered thinking, "leading like a woman" thinking into the discourse of peace? This can include integration of Olof Palme's concept of common security and Sun Tzu's thinking about what you do when you want peace in "The Art of War". There is a need to delegitimize war without creating sitting duck states that will be open to the war mongering states, at a time when we have not convinced everyone about the destructive impact of war.

We need to replicate experiences of successful women peacekeeping efforts. Whilst there is evidence to suggest challenges with woman peacekeeping, particularly in the Sudan, there is also evidence of successful woman peace- keeping and lasting impact of woman peacekeeping in various parts of the world. As such these should be analyzed for understanding why those missions succeeded. Some of the evidence of women's involvement in peace keeping missions can be summarized as follows:

- Long lasting peace where peace agreements include women

- Can prevent peace e.g. the best-known and most celebrated diplomatic agreement to be settled in 2015 was not to put an end to a war, but to prevent one. After many years of failed negotiations and decades of enmity, the Republic of Iran and a group of countries formed by the United States, Russia, China, France, the United Kingdom, and Germany reached a historic deal to curb Iran's nuclear programme. Women were involved in this deal.

- Can reach agreement when women are involved

- Women are persistent in taking peace efforts forward

- Better consensus building skills

- Peace keeping missions that involve women are more effective e.g. also help with GBV and children/ family issues.

Chapter 13: Leading Like a Woman in Non-profit Spaces

1. Introduction

The Non-Profit Sector has been around since Abraham's times, but in those days, it depended on individual consciences. It started being a sector in the West from biblical foundations. In China, it started from kinship and family structures. In Africa it was weaved into the norms, values and culture of communal society which was geared at sharing equitably. (Please refer to Chapter 3 which reflects on "ubuntu").

Whilst the non-profit sector has interesting vicissitudes in terms of origin in different geographic spaces and in different aeons and eras; it has evolved to a standard which one might say is dominated and underpinned by Western values of charity in 2019.

2. Women in Non-Profit Spaces

In the current period one can say that, whilst they are the number one beneficiary and many employees in the non-profit sector, women are still a minority when it comes to the leadership even in the non-profit sector. We are told that only 12-14 % of women are estimated to be leading the larger non- profit sector in the United States and about 27% is leading the larger non- profit sector in the United Kingdom and between 10-20% is estimated to be leading the non-profit sector in Africa. This indicates that desired change will be hard to come by, if desired change is to eradicate inequality and en- trench genuine respect for every human being and their rights across the globe, accompanied by equitable and decent living conditions.

The 21st century has revealed that even in these spaces, women continue to experience GBV for example sexual harassment. The latest most public indicator of this has been found at Oxfam.

Case Study

Whilst these infractions of acceptable behavior in the workplace occurred around 2010 or so during the response to the Haiti earthquake crisis, the responses of Oxfam are recorded as starting in 2011 and not far-reaching enough. In February 2018, the UK Times newspaper reported on sexual misconduct inside Oxfam and this led to a more vibrant response in the form of a 10-point plan which included the set- ting up of a high level, independent Commission of Enquiry into Sexual Misconduct, Accountability and Culture Change.

Several management staff members resigned whilst others who are junior were sacked after these issues came to light. We have learnt that these actions are monitored and reported on every three months. In addition, more resources have been made available (over 3 million Euros) for the response to GBV inside Oxfam. Because of these developments, funders were very reluctant to donate to Oxfam, which lost over 14 million in donor funding because of this scandal.

The case study above indicates that cases of human rights and sexual abuses are occurring in spaces that have largely been considered bastions of human right advancement. We also learn that even in these spaces, responses are not as thoroughgoing as they should and could be. In addition, the media played an important role in this case to place the issue in the public space and forcing a more effective response from Oxfam. We also learnt that accountability of the leadership of institutions can be achieved as we saw in the resignations of some managers. The case study exposes the need for institutions to balance their impact with internal respect for the human rights of their people and respect for their people within the organization. This weakness of caring only about impact on our intended beneficiaries is not found only in the non-profit sector, but it is quite widespread beyond this sector.

The non-profit sector is also a microcosm of society. If the society is virulently patriarchal, chances are the non-profit sector will have some indicators of toxic masculinity and patriarchy.

Case Study

In one NGO in Africa, the new Director who was a woman was able to have a collegial interaction with her new team and plan a useful strategy for taking the NGO forward. The collective had looked at whether the vision and mission of the NGO was still relevant and had agreed that indeed it was still relevant. They proceeded to agree on the interventions that would propel the organization forward.

The implementation of the strategy went well where it looked at the benefits of the personnel. It did not go well when personnel had to make some adjustments. The women in this NGO tended to have higher qualifications than the men, but the men were earning the same as women who had higher qualifications and they wanted higher pay if they improved their qualifications to those held by the women.

Women raised sexual harassment complaints informally and refused to raise these complaints officially, as all referred to victims who had left the organization. The Board of the NGO was mostly male, and the members did not agree on how the challenges of the NGO must be handled. The Director resigned after a couple of years.

This case study shows how toxic masculinity and patriarchy dominate non- profit workplaces as well. It really is very disappointing to find that even in these spaces' women are still a minority. They have not been able to support each other even where patriarchy is dealing unjustly with them. This case study also shows the fear that women have about raising issues of sexual harassment and GBV, fair remuneration etc. even as a principle and a key component of a workplace code of good conduct.

3. Leading like a woman in Non-Profit Spaces

Leadership and governance in the non-profit sector must consider these few suggestions to desirably lead like a woman:

- The quantity, numbers and percentages of woman leadership must be increased in the non-profit sector and they must be paid at the same rate as male counterparts. The data indicates that women earn between a quarter and a third less than their male counterparts at management level.

- Gender-transformation must be part and parcel of the culture and ethos changes that occur in the non-profit sector, the better to eliminate toxic masculinities and patriarchy.

- Ongoing conscious, targeted and focused conversations, workshops, seminars about the desirable changes that must take place in the non-profit sector so that no-one feels alienated, oppressed, neglected, dehumanized in the non-profit sector. Consciousness building must be an ongoing activity within the non-profit sector.

- Prioritization of poor beneficiaries and engendering of development programs because these beneficiaries are almost always women be- cause of the women's economic and power position in society.

- Engendering the tools that we use for monitoring and tracking impact on the lives of intended beneficiaries, the majority of whom are women.

- Investigating how working conditions can change in the non-profit sector to benefit women who work within the sector.

1. Introduction

The concept of traditional leadership that will be used here is one that is taken in a very generic sense from South Africa. Traditional leadership in the South African context has been largely a male domain, with some exceptions where a mother would be a regent on behalf of her young son, and also in the case of the rain queens. For the most part, traditional leadership has meant male leadership.

In the history of traditional leadership in South Africa, whilst men were kings, except in the case of the rain queen, women still played a very important role in the royal household and their influence could not be ignored. It must be made clear in this text that this also depended on the individual character, strength and charisma of those women. It was not provided for in the social and political fabric of a South African community.

It is very interesting to look at traditional leadership and eco-socio-political life in pre-colonial times and look at it again in post-colonial times. In pre- colonial times, there were roles set aside for men, others that were set aside for women, and others that were set aside for growing boys and growing girls as part of preparation for adult roles. It may be self-evident and unnecessary to say that people engaged in all that industry and business for the sole purpose of promoting life and that communally and collectively. In different roles each person was playing a role in the preservation and promotion of life, including kings. In post-colonial times, the role of traditional leadership changed.

There was a marked decline in the role and nature of consultation (imbizo). It became an area where the king (traditional leaders) makes decrees and issues instructions and not a place of exchange and collective decision making. A wide gap developed between the traditional leader and the people. The traditional leader of 2019 can no longer contribute to setting up a new family, because the material conditions have changed, everyone has been dispossessed of their belongings and impoverished. The gap between men and women widened because men had to carry the entire load of providing for their families whereas before women were providers for their families as well, who provided food through agricultural activities. The introduction of Victorian ideals to Southern Africa had created socio-economic chaos and a new dependency for African women.

The aim of this section is not to idealize and romanticize life in pre-colonial times. It is to show that the inequalities that existed in pre-colonial times were manageable and tended to be understood within a broader communal and survivalist frame. In post-colonial times these were sharpened by shifting material conditions and calcified into what we have today a toxic masculine and patriarchal culture, with African men attributing Victorian ideals to "our culture".

In fact, women did not take kindly to land dispossession through various edicts and proclamations all over Africa. In South Africa they organized various protests and organized themselves as the Bantu Women's League.

2. Women in Traditional Leadership Spaces

Traditional leadership spaces tend to be rural and peri-urban spaces where there is no energy, sanitation and clean water infrastructure. The impact of these shortages is felt by women who carry the burden of reproductive labor. In 2019 there are more clinics and schools; but these are still not enough to cater for the needs of the communities and questions of quality service have still not been answered sufficiently and the burden of inadequate health services in these spaces is carried by women. Most women in traditional spaces do not have Matric. The majority of the few who are educated have gone up to Grade 9. This greatly diminishes chances of decent employment and relegates many of them to precarious living where one can have a piece (read casual) job for a day, sometimes.

Women in traditional spaces tend not to have a voice. If there is a voice, then it is muted because women are not encouraged to speak when their husbands are present in a community meeting. The man speaks for her as well. A point to make here is that women participated in community meetings in pre-colonial times, but were excluded physically in the post- colonial period. Facilitating community discussions on GBV for example is not an easy task because men tend to dominate these discussions. Women need to be consulted separately and there is a need for them to be capacitated on speaking up about issues that affect them.

The spouses of traditional leaders are also neglected and devalued, even more so when they become older. Lack of formal structure for the spouses within the House of Traditional Leaders was raised as one of the barriers to promoting the women's agenda within the Traditional context. There are no genuine forums that can allow for a woman's voice in traditional spaces in the districts, provinces and nationally. There is no common policy and practice regarding the role of spouses within their tribal communities.

The state does not recognize spouses for an example, during State events only the Traditional Leaders will be catered for, but not their wives. The is- sue of financial and social security benefits for spouses is another serious matter that is ignored, whereas in terms of recognized cultural customs they are not allowed to work but to depend on the Traditional Leader's salary which it is not enough for the entire family.

Spouses also don't participate in or contribute to the traditional councils which make it difficult to promote the women's agenda. The women's agenda on issues of health, sanitation, energy, climate change, safety and GBV, education, living conditions, economic development etc needs a driver in traditional communities and possible drivers of these programs could be the spouses, in the absence/ blockage of women's own agency.

Another critical matter is the maintenance of the spouse and her younger children when the Traditional Leader has passed on. The new Traditional Leader who takes over the throne will receive the stipend from government and support his family.

Spouses complain that they do not have marriage certificates, although they are legally married in terms of the Customary Marriages Act and it is difficult for them to request the Traditional Leaders to register their marriages with the state as per the dictates of the statute because at times Traditional Leaders marry more than one wife without the consent of the first wife and may have reservations about registering any of the wives. Polygamy is oppressive to the wives of Traditional Leaders because they are not equal to their husbands.

As South Africa is a leader in GBV and femicide, the situation of women in rural areas needs urgent attention. The South African Parliament has passed the Traditional Courts Act which is a legislation that allows for customary or traditional law to be used in areas allotted to traditional leaders. The voice of gender activists and women's rights activists was ignored in favor of a cosmetic alignment with the progressive South African Constitution; BUT experience with traditional leadership in South Africa has shown that:

- Women, men and families have been physically assaulted at the instruction of traditional leaders

- Women have been dispossessed of their homes and inheritance by unethical male members of their families with the co-operation of traditional leaders

- Traditional leaders have been silent and unresponsive when crimes of harassment have been perpetrated against woman-headed house- holds which has led to some women abandoning their homes and be- longings in fear for their safety and others have usurped their belongings without any response from traditional leaders

- Traditional leaders have been vocal about the unacceptability of gender non-conforming people in their areas

- Some traditional leaders have led their communities in a democratic and developmental manner, which we highly commend, whilst some used these offices for individual as opposed to community gain

In short, this Traditional Courts Act will perpetuate the oppression of women in traditional communities. The clauses of the Act that allow for citizens to choose the option of not using a traditional court may be the reason for certain citizens to be victimized and expelled from their communities. The CGE mandate has also been extended in this legislation. The constant ex- tension of the CGE mandate without commensurate increase in its budget is setting the CGE up for failure. All these issues were raised in the consultative process, but the balance of forces when this Bill was tabled in Parliament, appears to have been anti-women, misogynistic and deaf to the cries of rural women and gender equality activists.

3. Leading like a woman in Traditional Leadership Spaces

Leaders in traditional spaces need to acknowledge the fact that traditional leadership spaces are oppressive to women mostly because of Victorian ideals that have crept into "traditional culture". As such they need to constantly critique how customary law and culture militates against women's rights to equality, dignity, freedom of choice and freedom to be.

Leaders in traditional spaces must engage regularly and meaningfully with women's structures in their communities to understand the strategic and practical needs of women in those communities.

Leaders in traditional spaces need to develop their own understanding about gender dynamics, gender equality and gender transformation the better to lead in inclusive and people-building ways.

Leaders in traditional spaces must target poverty eradication in a gender mainstreamed manner in their communities because most of the poor any- where in the world are women.

Leaders in traditional spaces must work for public infrastructure that pro- motes access to knowledge, information and communication, access to jobs and income generating opportunities, access to markets, access to movement of goods and people, local economic development and social development.

Women, feminists and gender activists in these communities still need to build a movement that will transform these spaces meaningfully and work towards the abolition of the Traditional Courts Act so that people, especially women, in the rural areas can enjoy the human rights that are enshrined in Chapter 2 of the South African Constitution.

Chapter 15: Tricks to watch out for if you are a leader who is leading like a woman

1.0 Introduction

Because of patriarchy, racism and prejudice if you are a woman/ non- white/ disabled/ gender non-conforming leader there are many issues that you need to look out for, because in general men and women, may tend to have very little hope for your leadership.

Because people are so dynamic and interesting, some of them will genuinely not want you to succeed and they can consciously or unconsciously set traps and create unnecessary challenges for you.

The following small bag contains a short list of tricks that you must watch out for.

2.0 Bag of tricks

When you come into a place as a new person, you will have an information drought. Most workplaces provide an orientation session for their new incumbents. You may find that in these sessions you are getting information, but it is not **all** the information you need to understand your environment. In more toxic environments, there isn't even an orientation. You are sup- posed to sink or swim. In such spaces you keep discovering the real deal, and it can take you more than 5 years to discover the real deal in such toxic spaces. Sometimes people think that they are helping by withholding information especially about the history of the organization but that is false, because knowledge **is** power.

The other bag of tricks is disinformation. With disinformation, you can do a lot of things. Part of disinformation is telling complete untruths about a situation, in the context of leadership, we talk about an utter collapse of the organization, company, government or institution under this leadership. Or the total opposite, as required by the tellers of this story. In disinformation, you can also attribute your own negative and destructive thoughts to some- one perceived to be an ally of your targeted leader. I call this *attribution*. It is hoped in that retelling that the targeted leader will view that ally negatively and thus loses that alliance. This is a favored trick in high stakes environments such as business and politics, where the losses are never small.

The other trick that is favoured by such individuals is carrying stories from one corner to another. This is closely aligned to disinformation because the stories may be true, half-true or false, it does not matter, the aim is to create a bit of chaos. All this is aimed consciously or unconsciously at unsettling leadership. Others come to share what is being said about you. Others go and share with others what you think of them.

The other trick is feeding leaders untrue stories about a particularly strong character, very common if that strong character is a woman or black or gen- der non-conforming. This is aimed at building a very negative perception about that individual in the mind of the leader. Leaders really must test all the information that is given to them about people in their absence before acting on that information.

At other times you find skilled manipulators. These are skilled at manipulating stakeholders to see things only from their perspective. This trick is usually very successful for a short while. Depending on the dynamics in that setting, the truth does come out eventually. A great example of this dynamic is in all the companies whose share price collapsed after a previously hidden truth came out. The victims in such transactions are the investors (big and small) who were manipulated to see opportunity and prospects in a dead company, who were manipulated to invest in a shell of a company whose value was eroded by unethical practices. Here the skilled manipulators can corrupt the auditors to release fictional financial reports.

When you are a woman leader, you must be very cautious because some men will use anything to create a negative cloud around you and your leadership. This can be done through amorous approaches that are designed to destroy you. When this fails, perpetrators can also create an impression that there **is** a sexual relationship with you. This can also be positioned as authoritative and destructive gossip about your love life. These things emerge from the depths of patriarchal hell and are informed by problematic as- sumptions of ownership and authority over women's bodies and lives that random men often claim over women, and label it as "locker room" talk. All these are meant to weaken your impact as a woman leader.

Many of the tricks in the bag of tricks always collapse, some sooner than others. Many of these are created to stop the flow of communication between a leader and certain parties. If the leader is bold and courageous, it is not easy to block her from talking even to "perceived enemies". The tricks there- fore collapse when there is balanced communication with everyone and all the stakeholders in a context.

Chapter 16: Counsel for Leaders who want to Lead Like a Woman

Everyone has strong points and weak points and usually people have serious blinders when it comes to their more serious weaknesses. Leaders who lead like a woman must be able to take feedback about their weaknesses well. This requires that you get more information from the person who is giving you feedback the better to understand the perceived weakness.

Some people get promotions when they are not mature or ripe enough to ascend to leadership. This often comes out in their inability to be self-aware about their strengths and their weaknesses. This can manifest in a manner where the leader is dealing with issues in an inconsistent manner, changing a point of view within two minutes because they have been called out for trying to please strong viewpoints. These leaders are shaky and afraid to take decisions. Yet in others this can manifest in a style of leadership that is Thatcherite, who was known for not taking suggestions from others and was resolute in her campaigns to clean the United Kingdom, to the point of making her party very unpopular and paving the way for Tony Blair.

All leaders are not knowledgeable about everything that they will come across whilst undertaking the task of leadership. It is strongly recommended that leaders make a habit of continuous professional development so that they can always add value to themselves and make a more successful job of leading any enterprise or institution with more information and knowledge. Self-development is your friend if you hope or want to lead one day, or even if you find yourself in leadership by default. You cannot hope to be a General Secretary of an organisation who is not studying further on subjects that are relevant for your type of organisation. You cannot expect to be a successful Chairperson of a Board if you do not study further on issues that are relevant to your enterprise or to governance generally. Oftentimes, peo- ple fall into leadership because of place and time, but this is no excuse not to invest in yourself so that you grow into the position you fell into. Many times, men have not been happy about further education, and this is a problem as they cannot grow by using the same old tricks.

As you grow as a leader there are weaknesses that will be revealed to you without the aid of anyone. Those revelations direct you to what you need to change about yourself to become a better leader. So, this means that as a leader, especially if you want to lead like a woman; you must be alert to note these revelations and not just let them pass without you doing something about what has been revealed to you. This is important because only changed people can change the world. Do not expect to change the world when you have not changed or if you are unwilling to change.

Leaders who lead like a woman are usable in the leadership space because the power that is given to them is controlled, managed and held with great care. They understand that power and authority at their disposal is not for subjugating people, but it is for growing and building people. They under- stand that power must be **used,** and it must be used to advance our institutions, our organizations, our departments, our governance etc. Cowardly leadership leads from fear and seeks only to maintain the status quo, and not to improve anything.

Leaders must have big picture thinking, they must have big visions. This is very important although the reality of budgets is that they are always limited. Big picture thinking when married to a limited budget can still give you something great e.g. you can implement your big picture in small chunks or you can pare it down but still get a great result if you do not lose the focus on a big impact even on a small budget.

Leaders who lead like a woman must be vigilant against tokenism. Tokenism is being given a position as an affirmative action intervention, whilst not giv- en the power and authority to execute the leadership task. Tokenism does not allow you to institute the changes that are sorely needed by the organi- sation, institution or company. Tokenism means that you are a decoration, only to be seen to be in that position, with no impact. Leaders who lead like a woman are ethical leaders; they should consider other options when con- fronted with such conditions.

Leaders who lead like a woman must be cognisant of the constant ebbs and flows in the understanding of gender equality, gender equity, gender justice, socio-economic justice and commensurate praxis. Leaders who lead like a woman must be vigilant and ensure that these ebbs and flows get the appropriate response that protects equality, fairness and justice for the most vulnerable. It means that consistency may be a saving grace for all organisations and it can help organisations create and maintain the culture and the impact that they desire.

Gender mainstreaming and gender transformation are essential weapons in the arsenal of a leader who leads like a woman. These two approaches help in levelling the playing fields in favour of the vulnerable, discriminated and marginalised. These impact on and help eradicate patriarchy and other ex- clusionary beliefs and practices in an organisation, institution, company or society. Gender mainstreaming is a policy tool developed out of dissatisfaction with how Women in Development (WID) projects integrated women's concerns. WID projects were viewed as "add on" of women's concerns, rather than integrating them into the mainstream or transforming broader societal and institutional contexts. In the 1980s it developed into the Gender and Development (GAD) paradigm that attempted to be more transformative by including women's concerns into mainstream policy making. When a shift occurred from GAD to gender mainstreaming in the 1990s it was indicative of a language change as well as the globalization of the agenda to address gendered outcomes and institutional change.

Gender mainstreaming is the process of assessing the implications for women and men of any planned action, including legislation, policies or programs in all areas and at all levels. It has been adopted globally as a strategy to ensure that gender equality is one of the outcomes of all development interventions in social, economic and political spheres. The aim of gender mainstreaming is to eradicate gender discrimination and oppression, attain gender equality and transform society. Gender transformation utilizes gender mainstreaming to effect the changes that may be necessary to ensure that men, women and other genders experience different environments fairly and justly.

Gender mainstreaming must include the following interventions that are suggested by McKinsey & Company and often proposed by the Commission for Gender Equality (CGE) to institutions in the gender transformation hearings:

"Make gender diversity a top board CEO priority. Senior leaders should develop and enforce a cohesive gender diversity transformation strategy, own the communication about this transformation, monitor progress and lead the change.

Anchor gender diversity strategies in a compelling business case. Communicate the business case simply and clearly so that employees understand how to link their individual interests to the success of a gender diversity transformation program.

Confront limiting attitudes toward women in the workplace. Address unconscious bias by educating all employees, reviewing and changing processes. For example, recruitment and performance reviews to make decision-making more objective; include men in gender diversity transformation initiatives; conduct surveys to understand what the limiting attitudes are.

Implement a fact-based gender diversity strategy. Develop a strategy based on solid gender diversity metrics and address the root causes of lower shares of women's representation. Metrics include pay levels of female versus male staff, women's attrition rates and reasons for exiting, the percentage of women receiving promotions and in which roles/functions, and organizational health metrics (such as job satisfaction, perceptions of meritocracy, work-life balance, and desire for advance- ment)."

Leaders who lead like a woman need to study the environment they are in so that they emerge with approaches that can work in that environment. In healthy organizations the process of studying the environment can be concluded in 6-12 months.

This is a much more challenging process in toxic spaces. Toxic spaces thrive on secrecy and on disempowering the leadership, which is why leaders can find themselves in the learning curve six years after assuming leadership. This is particularly prevalent in government institutions where the political leader is always changing, but the bureaucracy remains the same. The only thing that grows under these conditions is the power of the bureaucracy and not societal or citizen's benefits. There is a need to look at how one restructures things there to allow for more transparency, democracy and accountability.

Leaders who lead like women have a moral duty to build up women and other groups that are discriminated against such as youth. Mentoring should be one of the key responsibilities of leaders who lead like a woman.

Leaders who lead like a woman must double check all the claims of hard work that "people" make in the workplace. In some cases, men exaggerate the work they do as well as the impact. In some cases, men use friendly women (not their staff) to get the desirable results e.g. a complete report, a policy proposal, a speech they are supposed to prepare for their boss, a master's thesis etc. I hope that this is not a general thing, but this has been known to happen and I hope to discourage this practice through this book.

Leaders who want to lead like a woman and who want to be effective leaders need to know that they cannot learn the knowledge, skills and values of leadership from the wrong people. Who **are** the wrong people? The wrong people are people who are always shouting at their subordinates, are people who will do anything to maintain their positions, are people who are unethi- cal, are people who only see things from their perspective, are people who say one thing and do another, are people who lack courage, are people who lack self-awareness, are people who fail to be accountable and blame others for everything, are people who lack confidence, are people who have no compunction about putting others under the bus, are people who lack stewardship.

Leaders who lead like a woman have a higher task to promote woman leadership in the spaces that they occupy. It may appear to be a simple matter to get women to support other women in the office of leader; but patriarchy has showed us that it's not so. Some women do not even understand why we need to have women leaders let alone, support them. A lot of work needs to be done by gender activists, feminists and champions of egalitarianism to ensure that no human being is negated, dehumanized or made to be and feel less than other humans including making sure that women are acknowledged as naturally as men in the role of leadership.

Leaders who lead like a woman need to ensure that the systems that help to protect each and every person e.g. an inclusive/ integrated human rights framework are protected and guarded jealously so that women can feel free to be, to speak and to participate and engage.

In many spaces women find themselves compelled to manage, control and limit themselves unfairly and to their detriment; whilst men can freely be, speak and engage including invading spaces that should by rights protected for women's safety. This lackadaisical approach to maintenance of the systems referred to here often curtails women's interest in participating or in leading. When people's rights are not protected equally, the biggest losers are often women, children and other vulnerable groups.

Last, but not least, leaders who lead like a woman are discouraged from having "work wives" or "work husbands" as well as any real sexual relation- ships in the workplace. No favorites in the workplace. This serves leaders well in their positions because male leaders, female leaders and other leaders have to be objective at all times. Such things can be manageable until they are not manageable and blow up in the face of a leader.

ISBN NUMBER: 9798593440013

References http://www.langston.edu/
https://courses.lumenlearning.com

https://online.stu.edu/
https://www.greenleaf.org
https://davidburkus.com www.forbes.com
https://www.success.com/ https://hbr.org
https://blog.zef.fi/
https://www.emergenetics.com
www.womentakingthelead.com
www.bus.umich.edu
www.entrepreneur.com www.cge.org.za
https://css.ethz.ch
www.servicewomen.com
www.buzzfeednews.com
www.theatlantic.com
www.oxfordresearchgroup.org.uk
www.ngopulse.org www.theguardian.com
www.oxfam.org.uk

(All the sites above were accessed in 2019, between 1 February and 5 July 2019)
McKinsey Report, Women Matter Africa, 2016
Sun Tzu, The Art of War, 2013, The Winds of Japan Shop

The Bible
Zingiswa Losi, "Reflecting on the women's struggle in South Africa and the world" 22 August 2018, Speech at Worker Education Conference

Contact the author: leadinglikeawoman@gmail.com